Blue Ridge Wine Excursions

Explore the Monticello Wine Trail

Andrea E. Saathoff

i

Cover illustration by Elizabeth Flood

ISBN-13: 978-1499296433

For more information about custom editions, special sales, and premium and corporate purchases, please contact Blue Ridge Wine Excursions at 434-531-5802 or info@blueridgewineexcursions.com

Manufactured in the United States of America

Dedicated to those who make their livelihood in the Virginia wine industry, to my talented wine trail team, and my husband Greg for his encouragement and support.

"Wine is the most civilized thing in the world."
                                        -Earnest Hemingway

Table of Contents

Foreword

By: Richard Leahy

Welcome to the Monticello American Viticultural Area (AVA)! This wine region of the upper Virginia Piedmont includes Albemarle and Nelson counties and parts of Greene and Orange counties in the heart of the Central Virginia countryside. Two thirds of the U.S. population lives within a day's drive of Charlottesville. In fact, this small University City, renowned for its culture, arts, and leisurely lifestyle, is less than a three-hour drive from, and serves as a scenic complement to the federal and military seats of power in the Washington Metropolitan and Tidewater areas respectively. The Monticello AVA is also the only wine region in the country host to three homes of former U.S. Presidents (two of whom were Founding Fathers), and each of the three is also host to its own wine festival.

A wide range of people, from consumers who tried Virginia wine 20 years ago (and were not impressed), to leading world wine authorities agree that the Virginia wines of today are world-class. In 2010, the influential London-based Circle of Wine Writers made Virginia their official wine region destination and came away highly impressed with both the wines and the state itself as a travel destination. In 2011 the annual Wine Bloggers Conference was held in Charlottesville, introducing many of the attendees to Virginia wine for the first time. In 2012 Wine Enthusiast listed Virginia among its "Top Ten" wine destinations in the world. In October of that year, at the first Virginia Wine Summit, Steven Spurrier (a member of the Circle of Wine Writers), whose landmark blind tasting of French vs. California wines in 1976 was featured in the movie *Bottle Shock*, remarked in his keynote address that today he prefers Virginia wines to those of California categorically.

Supporting regional wine is viewed as progressive and "green" by consumers concerned about the carbon footprint of buying goods from thousands of miles away. As a natural part of the "locavore" movement, it's appropriate to seek out and drink local wines to support local agriculture, but the rising excellence of Virginia wine means that buying local doesn't mean sacrificing quality.

Since its delineation in 1987, the Monticello AVA has won more top awards for Virginia wines than any other Virginia viticultural area. Here in the rolling hills of Central Virginia, which bear a strong resemblance to the Italian Piedmont; vines have a long growing season, lots of sunshine and rain, good air and water drainage and produce a diverse range of fine wines. These range from the esoteric white Rhone grape Viognier to the well-known Cabernet Franc and Merlot Bordeaux grapes, to the lesser-known Petit Verdot, Tannat and even more esoteric white French grape, Petit Manseng. Looking around at many handsome views of the nearby Blue Ridge Mountains and other hills, we can easily understand why Thomas Jefferson enthused in a letter to John Dortie in 1781, "Wine, being among the earliest luxuries in which we indulge ourselves, it is desirable that it should be made here and we have every soil, climate and aspect of the best wine countries..."

Most fans of Virginia wine, either in-state or in nearby states, like to experience Virginia wine in person by visiting the wineries. With the rise of "stay-cations" in recent years and also the phenomenon of "wiking" (hiking on trails near wineries, then ending at one or more wineries), as well as thanks to the buzz about Virginia wine, winery visitation in Virginia keeps rising. The regional wine industry is at least as much about destination tourism as a product in a bottle. As many tourists now visit Virginia for its wineries as for birding and golfing (2% or 55 from a total of 2,775 based on a sample survey by the VA Tourism Corp. in 2011). A source at the VTC explains, "The Virginia Wine experience has really grown the past three years in terms of visitor comments, spreading the word and wanting to experience it firsthand." Statewide there has been an increase of 700,000 winery visitors over the last five years, according to the Virginia Wine Board Marketing Office.

As a long-time Charlottesville resident and the author of a recent, comprehensive book on Virginia wine (*Beyond Jefferson's Vines*), I can wholeheartedly say that the best and most memorable way to appreciate the wines of the Monticello AVA and its two wine trails is to make plans to visit them personally. Wineries in Virginia have learned that despite the rapid rise of wine quality in the last decade, what's in the bottle is only part of what they offer. What you get when you taste the wines at the source is a fun, educational and esthetic experience in a beautiful, memorable and relaxed environment.

Between the wineries of the Monticello and Appellation Wine Trails, you'll discover the impressive diversity of wineries, from some of the largest (Prince Michel, Early Mountain, Barboursville and Horton) to some of the smallest in the state (Mountfair, Stinson, Glass House and Moss); some of the oldest (Barboursville) to some of the newest (Stinson and Moss); those that are noted for large public events and weddings (Veritas and Pippin Hill) and those that are small and intimate. You'll also enjoy the diversity in design, architecture and scenic views from the spare utilitarian production focus of Virginia Wineworks, to the calm green design of Blenheim, to the North Coast modernity of Pollak, to the amazing views from King Family, Stinson, Moss and Veritas.

Another part of the fun diversity is the product line. Some producers specialize; Cardinal Point has many manifestations of Cabernet Franc but also makes a Vinho Verde-style wine called simply "Green." Glass House makes a chocolate (cocoa powder) infused port-style norton called "Melio de Sesso" (I'll let them translate for you), as well as a "passito-style" Barbera made from dried grapes. Mountfair specializes in red Bordeaux *blends*, while Veritas is passionate about varietal Petit Verdot and two fine but very different styles of Sauvignon Blanc. Keswick Vineyards makes the state's only Verdejo (a white aromatic Spanish grape), and three labels of Viognier.

Best of all, you can talk to the friendly winery tasting room staff (which can sometimes include owners themselves) and discover their passion that led them to take the plunge and make wine in Virginia. What did they do before, and aside from a love of wine, what was it that made them become producers, and why here of all places? The stories are many and diverse but have all resulted in the owners investing much of themselves, their vision and passion into their operations, all for your benefit.

For heading out on the wine trails in the Monticello AVA, this book is a handy and valuable resource, giving you a brief but detailed summary of all the local wineries including profiles of the owners, what they grow and produce, and the personal differences they have in style, size and products. You can quickly get to the heart of what makes each winery tick, and the six different writers give the book a nice variety of voices. It's also very helpful for those who want to learn a bit more that handy resources are included in the back, from books and websites to wine-related terms and a list of grapes grown in Virginia and their characteristics.

Blue Ridge Wine Excursions is an experienced, locally owned and operated tour business specializing in introducing small, private groups to the wineries of the Monticello AVA, and the seven writers of the winery profiles also double as Wine Trail Guides for these excursions. You can see the attention to detail and love of the subject they have in reading the profiles in this book, which makes a great reason to experience both the guides and their subjects in person on one of their tours.

Many graduates of the University of Virginia, returning to Charlottesville to re-visit the area after years of living elsewhere, have been charmed to find the rise of the vibrant local wine business, and use the services of Blue Ridge Wine Excursions to re-discover the region in a new light. In 2012 Patrick, an alumnus of U.Va, and his wife, Mary Ann Drinan, visited the area. Patrick contacted me through my blog (www.richardleahy.com) and asked if I could help him find some resources on Jefferson and wine, as he wanted to write a book on the many interests of Jefferson. I suggested a personal tour with Blue Ridge Wine Excursions and they not only learned much about Jefferson's vision for American viticulture, but enjoyed experiencing how Jefferson's own countryside had finally realized his vision of producing world-class wine, and described the tour as "truly unique and wonderful." A quick check of TripAdvisor.com for ratings of Blue Ridge Wine Excursions will yield results with impressive and consistently high ratings.

I hope you enjoy learning more about the Monticello

AVA, its wineries and trails, and make plans to tour it personally soon.

Cheers,
Richard Leahy
Author, *Beyond Jefferson's Vines*

Introduction
By: Andrea E. Saathoff

In the thirty years since my husband and I arrived in Charlottesville, I have been amazed at how this area has grown and changed. Of all the changes, perhaps the most extraordinary has been the development of the Virginia wine community. Our region is now a top destination for wine lovers, as well as for those who simply enjoy the ambiance of a small, beautiful university town, rich in history.

My own introduction to the Virginia wine industry came in a circuitous way. When one of our children married, we wanted to surprise the new couple with a chauffeured vintage limousine ride from the University Chapel. Without any local options available, we were delighted when a family friend offered to drive the bride and groom in his vintage limousine. The car and the experience were wonderful. After the nuptials, I decided to make a business providing gracious service in beautiful vintage cars for weddings. The response was overwhelming.

Because area vineyards are some of the best venues in the country for weddings and celebrations, it wasn't long before people began asking if we would drive them out in modern vehicles for a day of wine exploration. Through referrals, word of mouth and people simply coming up to admire the beautiful cars at events, Blue Ridge Wine Excursions has become the top provider of private wine tours in the region. Over the past several years, we have been delighted to welcome visitors from all over the United States and international tourists from Europe, Africa, South America, Australia, as well as Asia.

The past thirty years have also seen an expansion

of our community's business and cultural offerings. The Virginia Festival of the Book and the Virginia Film Festival have attained national prominence. The renovation of the magnificent Paramount Theater has served as an anchor for the arts. Fine local cuisine, an explosion in the theater and music scenes, a revitalization of Downtown, an upswing in U.Va's sports programs, and both national and international headlining entertainment at the John Paul Jones Arena are just a few of the remarkable developments over the last three decades.

In addition to enjoying the sublime vistas and vintages in Virginia wine country, our guests appreciate the opportunity to walk the grounds of the University of Virginia, enjoy the historic Downtown Mall and Court Square, take a sunrise hot air balloon ride and find lodging in fine local hotels and bed and breakfasts. Steeped in history, Monticello, Montpelier and Ash Lawn are an architectural testament to the lives of our Founding Fathers. Indeed, many of our guests are so pleased with the offerings in our area that they extend their stays. Some may even make the decision that my husband and I made thirty years ago – to call it home.

The Monticello Wine Trail and the Appellation Wine Trail (whose name and spelling are often confused with the Appalachian Hiking Trail) are collaborative associations that continue to develop and grow. The coming decades promise an even richer tapestry of community and culture. Visitors have been lured by the area's natural beauty and hospitality since before Jefferson's time. As cultural and recreational opportunities continue to expand, the region's popularity as a tourist destination will only continue to grow.

In the process of learning about the wineries, my

Wine Trail Guides were often asked to provide background and insight into the area's fine wines and the people who create them. This book shares some of those wonderful stories about local history, natural beauty, entrepreneurial vision, and the wines that bring guests back to the area over and over.

The chapters that follow tell the stories of the people who make the Virginia wine industry what it is today. The diversity of backgrounds, philosophies and experiences showcases the mosaic that is our vibrant local wine community. We invite the reader to enjoy these stories and to join us on the Monticello Wine Trail!

Sincerely,

Andrea E. Saathoff

The History of Virginia Wine

By: Justin Stone

The history of wine in Virginia dates back to 1607 with the successful establishment of a colony at Jamestown by the Virginia Company. Early accounts of the abundance of native grape varietals sent back by Captain John Smith created a fervent desire to make wine in the New World. In 1619 the Virginia House of Burgesses passed Act 12, requiring each head of a household to plant ten vines and, "attain to the arte and experience of dressing a Vineyard." By most historical accounts, however, such attempts to make palatable wines failed. By 1768 the American colonies were exporting less than 13 tons of wine that, by most standards, on either side of the Atlantic, was undrinkable, due to the persistent foxiness, or musty aroma and taste associated with American grape varietals. Thomas Jefferson is famous for meticulously documenting his life-long failures of producing wine on his Monticello estate. Even Philip Mazzei, the Florentine noble and vintner who Jefferson called a close friend and neighbor, was so frustrated by the ground (and the Revolutionary War) that he eventually gave up all hope of seeing a successful vintage. Jefferson's vision of an American wine industry on par with that of Europe's would have to wait.

The 1800s proved to be a more fruitful era for Virginia wine. It was a controversial and misunderstood grape varietal known as a Norton, widely considered a hybrid of *V. vinifera* (European species) and *V. aestivalis* or *V. labrusca* (American species) that brought Virginia wine its first taste of prominence. The true genealogical origin and individual who discovered the grape remains shrouded by history but no one can dispute the role it played in introducing Virginian and American wine to the world market. By the mid 1850s, the Norton was the premier grape of Virginia, Missouri, and the Ohio River Valley, the three largest producers of wine prior to Prohibition. It surpassed other popular native grapes such as the Concord, Catawba, and Scuppernong in heartiness, complexity, and age-worthiness. At the extravagant 1873 Universal Exhibition in Vienna, a bottle of Norton from a vineyard in Hermann, Missouri claimed a gold medal among a field of twenty thousand bottles. Five years later at the Universal Exhibition in Paris, a bottle of Norton carried by the Monticello Wine Company, founded in 1873, earned a silver medal. Further successes of the company through the turn of the 20th century bolstered the city of Charlottesville, Virginia to declare itself the "the Capital of the Wine Belt in Virginia." However, these long awaited successes were rendered almost historically obsolete with the passage of the 18th Amendment in 1919 that began Prohibition.

Over the course of a decade and a half the memory of the wines and winemaking that had been so laboriously sought after for three hundred years was forgotten, the American palate for great wines thoroughly cleansed, and the established varietals nearly uprooted to extinction. After the production and sale of wine was made legal again in 1933 it would take over twenty years for vintners to create a market for themselves. By the 1950s, California had established itself as the premier wine-growing region in America. It would be another decade and a half before the potential of the Monticello region was tapped again.

When Gionni Zonin, head of an Italian wine enterprise dating back to 1820, decided that Virginia would be home to his New World vineyard, there were less than a dozen vineyards in the state. Most were private low-yield operations but few were having success growing *vinifera* vines. Gionni along with Gabriele Rausse, a talented young viticulturist, spent the early 1970s searching the Virginia countryside for the ideal setting for the winery before settling in 1976 on a nine hundred acre tract of land in Barboursville, Virginia. There, in the center of the Commonwealth's Piedmont region, these two men set to work planting and cultivating a wine enterprise that today produces wines of exceptional character. As a result of their innovation and pioneering, Barboursville is considered the birthplace of the modern wine industry in Virginia.

Over the course of the next twenty years other passionate and talented individuals joined in the cultivation of the bourgeoning industry with their erudite innovation, keen dedication, and willing acceptance of risk. These early pioneers of viticulture were faced with a geographical location known for its variant seasonal climate and little experience of successful grape growing. Dennis Horton, of Horton Vineyards, became a leading figure in varietal selection for the state after the mid-1980s when he became the first to commercially plant Viognier. The varietal is now grown by over seventy vineyards and considered a signature wine of Virginia. Today his tasting menu reads like a world's wine atlas, distinct for the presence of the ancient Rkatsiteli and the reclusive Norton. Jennifer McCloud, the resolute visionary behind Chrysalis Vineyards, has been spurring on her own revival of Norton since 1997 along with producing a stellar lineage of white wines. There is also Jim Law of Linden Vineyards whose tireless study and focus on the land matches that of the staunchest terroir-ist of Europe. He first began toiling in the Virginia soil in the early 1980s and now is among the top winemakers in the state.

The wines and recognition produced from the patient and dedicated efforts of these individuals became the catalyst for the eruption of Virginia wine. By 2000, over seventy wineries had planted grapes, pulled in a harvest, and released a first vintage. This number almost tripled in the decade that followed. According to the Virginia Wine Board, well over two hundred wineries will be releasing a 2014 vintage. With over four decades of experience and experimentation, there is a tangible excitement in the industry that Virginia wine is prepared to rise to an even higher level of quality.

International attention has already been garnered. Virginia wine is more readily available in the wine shops of London than New York. Young winemakers from around the world see Virginia as a premier training ground, full of potential and challenges. In 2011, an earthquake shook the region mid-summer and a hurricane assaulted the area during harvest. Add these uncertainties to the enduring threats of high humidity, frost and pests and Virginia becomes as tough a vintage driven region as any. However, its diversity of soils of limestone, clay, loam, and sand, along with its temperate climate with mountain and maritime influences proves irresistible to those willing to accept the risks. As winemakers and wine enthusiasts have recognized these nuances of Virginia's terroir, momentum has built towards a "tipping point" moment when Virginia wine would grow out from under California's shadow and proclaim its independence from Europe. That moment is near if not already here.

In 1808 Thomas Jefferson wrote in a letter, "We could, in the United States, make as great a variety of wines as are made in Europe, not exactly of the same kinds, but doubtless as good." Since its rebirth in the 1970s, the Virginia wine industry has sought an identity unique from its Old and New World forebears. Chardonnay and Cabernet Sauvignon are present but have not been championed as they were in the West. The other Bordeaux red grapes-Cabernet Franc, Merlot, Petit Verdot, and Malbec- have been singled out as possible state signatures but climate and common sense has brought them back together into uniquely Virginia-style blends of growing acclaim. Viognier matured into the state's premier white but petite manseng is gaining prominence as a grape grown nowhere else in the U.S. It took 204 years but Virginia vintners have found the variety and quality on which Jefferson so prophetically founded his passing dream. It is time for the dreams and dedication of others to carry Virginia wine forward.

Contact Us For a Wine Excursion

Let us escort you in comfort and style, as you taste some of Virginia's finest wines. Whether you are a couple looking for an intimate getaway, a small group celebrating a special occasion, or a business team looking for a creative outing, we'll take you there in style! Experience the natural beauty of the Blue Ridge Mountains or the charm of historic Charlottesville as you traverse the scenic countryside for a day of touring and tasting with our knowledgeable Wine Trail Guides. We offer a variety of modern vehicles for tours based on your group size.

- Custom Designed Itineraries
- Tasting Room Recommendations
- Winery Reservations (if required)
- Locally Catered Gourmet Lunch
- Experienced Wine Trail Guides

(434) 531-5802

info@blueridgewineexcursions.com

www.blueridgewineexcursions.com

Owners: Elizabeth and Tony Smith
Winemaker: Damien Blanchon
Year Established: 1990

Afton Mountain Vineyards

Albemarle County Natives Renew and Expand a Nelson County Hidden Gem.

By: Matt Brown

If their slogan "grapes don't grow in ugly places" is true, they have nothing to worry about: their vineyard is surrounded by beautiful vistas. Nestled at the foot of the Blue Ridge Mountains, the stunningly beautiful Afton Mountain Vineyards grows not only Chardonnay, Cabernet Sauvignon and Cabernet Franc, but also varietals not frequently seen in the Monticello AVA (American Viticultural Area): Gewürztraminer, Pinot Noir, Sangiovese and Albariño. Some of the vines at Afton Mountain date back to the 1970s: in an emerging wine region, it is rare to find vineyards of this age, and the fruit of these mature plantings adds to the character of the wine. These older vines have deeper, hardier roots, and even at nearly 40 years old, they are still in the prime of their lives.

Tony and Elizabeth Smith purchased the vineyard in 2009 to live out their dream of growing grapes and making wine. The transition from office work to fieldwork has been an adventure for the Smiths, and with the help of their skilled winemaker Damien Blanchon and viticulturist Brandon Bangley they have achieved local and national recognition for the fruits (and wines) of their labors.

Tony, who is in commercial real estate and teaches at the University of Virginia's Darden School of Business, and Elizabeth, who manages their personal real estate investments, have both put their years of experience to good use reinvigorating the vineyard and winery. Their son Hunter, who has his own entrepreneurial venture in the heart of Charlottesville called Champion Brewery, also serves as the marketing manager for Afton, making the vineyard a true family business. Even Brandon's dog Brussel Sprout does his part by keeping a watchful eye on the vines.

As in many family owned and operated vineyards in Virginia, every member of the Afton Mountain team from the Smiths to the tasting room staff takes great pride in their work. Winemaker Damien Blanchon, originally from Perpignan, France, comes from a long line of wine makers and viticulturists. Having studied in the South of France, Damien has strong roots in Old-World wine making styles. His youth and innovation have taken the wines at Afton Mountain to new heights, providing eager palates with exciting and creative wines. Now, in his seventh year making wine in Virginia, Damien has mastered the unique challenges of grape growing and winemaking in the Commonwealth.

The cozy tasting room at Afton Mountain is located in the renovated home of the former owners. Visitors settle into an inviting and relaxing space to enjoy not only tastings, but wine by the glass or bottle. Guests also enjoy an open patio and lovely pavilion with picnic tables and beautiful mountain views. Although the tasting room is stocked with a selection of meats, cheeses and other fine foods, guests are welcome to bring a picnic of their own to enjoy along with the wine and mountain views. On Saturday evenings during the summer months, "Afton After Hours" offers a chance to stay late and enjoy local music with a glass or two of a favorite Afton Mountain wine.

Of their many offerings, Afton Mountain is best known for their unique super-Tuscan blend, Festa Di Bacco. This smooth blend of Sangiovese and Bordeaux varietals is the flagship of their red wines. Afton's Pinot Noir is another exciting find. Fresh and fruit-forward, this Pinot Noir may remind you of Beaujolais Nouveau or a light Burgundy. Leaving Italy for Germany, Afton Mountain also produces excellent quality Gewurztraminer, which is dry and combines notes of citrus and spice. The 2010 vintage sparkling wine, Bollicine, is a blend of Pinot Noir and Chardonnay, vinted in the traditional méthode champenoise, and bottle aged for nearly two years on the sediment in the wine called lees. This wine is crisp, refreshing, and has a nice acidity, with prominent notes of toast and citrus.

Afton Mountain's beautiful setting, welcoming atmosphere, and excellent wines make it a memorable destination on any tour of Virginia wine country. In any season, and in any weather, Afton Mountain Vineyard is prepared to offer comfort and hospitality with every glass of wine.

Owners: Gianni and Silvana Zonin
Winemaker: Luca Paschina, joined Barboursville Vineyards
in 1990

Year Established: 1976

Barboursville Vineyards

"We are farmers because of our awe and gratitude for the character of this earth, and we are vintners because it is natural to desire to celebrate it, and to share it." — Gianni Zonin, 2006, Owner of Barboursville Vineyards.

Old World Traditions in the Land of Jefferson.
By: Justin Stone

The story of Barboursville Vineyards is inseparable from the story of the land. The estate was first cultivated by a prominent Virginia family in the late 1700s. It grew in wealth under the stewardship of James Barbour, the son of Thomas Barbour and Mary Pendleton Thomas, who would become the 19th Governor of Virginia and later Secretary of War under John Quincy Adams. Friendship and political allegiances with his colonial neighbors James Madison and Thomas Jefferson undoubtedly meant that James Barbour was a player in the formation of the new republic. Thomas Jefferson designed the stately brick and columned main house, which was home to the Barbour family until fire destroyed the building on Christmas, 1884. Though its sloping hills and rich soils are perfect for cultivating grapes, the land had to wait another century before its character and beauty was fully revealed in a glass of wine.

The American Bicentennial marked the real beginning of central Virginia's modern wine revolution. In the spring of 1976, Gianni Zonin, heir to his family's extensive 150-year-old wine enterprise in Northern Italy's Veneto region, acquired the Barboursville estate. Gianni and his wife Silvana decided on these 900 acres in the heart of the Virginia Piedmont because the natural beauty and kindness of the locals reminded them of their native Veneto. The Zonins brought on Gabrielle Rausse as Barboursville's first viticulturist, a man who remains a leading figure in Virginia wines. Together they set about reintroducing the European grapes, vitis vinifera, to Virginia and bringing to fruition a dream rooted in the earliest history of the Commonwealth. In 1979, the first bottle of wine cultivated from the ground at Barboursville was released.

Barboursville has remained true to the Italian traditions of wine and the adage that "wine is made in the vineyard." Through the 1980s the vineyard underwent many transformations, seeking varietals that made the most of the terroir. As the fields are not irrigated, the vines must also be allowed time to mature and grapes are not harvested from new vines for several years after planting.

In 1990, the current winemaker, Luca Paschina, came to Barboursville, and for the past 21 years he has been producing wines of exceptional character and style. His wines have received numerous national awards and international recognition. Barboursville Vineyards, a place rich in Virginia history and among the very first to awaken Jefferson's dream, is now considered to be one of the greatest treasures of the Monticello AVA.

An informative free tour is offered at Barboursville, with an educational and entertaining movie inside the

Octagon Room. Guests are free to roam the ruins, the family cemetery and the picnic areas. One of Virginia's finest restaurants, Palladio, is also on site. Their extraordinary offerings and attentive service create a memorable experience, and make it easy to spend the entire day at Barboursville, sampling, strolling, and dining.

The Zonins and Luca are committed to the belief that the reason for opening a bottle of wine is to find the most beautiful thing that can be drawn from the earth and to share it with others. This is their hope for each bottle of Barboursville wine.

© Elizabeth Flood

15

Owner: Dave Matthews
Winemaker: Kirsty Harmon
Year Established: 2000

Blenheim Vineyards
A Great Blend of Wine, Music, Art, and Community

By: Justin Stone

Blenheim Vineyards has blended the pleasures of wine, art, and community like few other places. Owned by renowned musician Dave Matthews and run by some of the most approachable staff in the business, the intersection of these spheres has become the center of Blenheim's philosophy.

In 2000, the final touches of Blenheim's two story joint tasting room and barrel room were completed. Designed by Dave Matthews and master craftsman William Johnson, this energy efficient hall features beautiful reclaimed timber framing a full southeastern façade of windows and skylights for natural lighting. A partial subterranean foundation helps maintain the consistent cool of the barrel room.

That same year, the first vines of Chardonnay, Cabernet Franc and Petit Verdot were planted. The first vintage was released in 2003, ushered in by Brad McCarthy, an experienced local winemaker. During Blenheim's early years, he and Peter Matthews, the first vineyard manager, established the grounds, the vines, and the principles that are at the heart of the winery today.

For the first five years after the vineyard opened, a private invitation was needed to visit Blenheim. Their wines established a cult-like following due to both this exclusivity and the association with Dave Matthews. However, in 2009, the winery opened its doors to the public and since then, Blenheim has been sharing its serene setting, approachable wines and gregarious staff with all who choose to visit.

Dave Matthews designs the labels for each vintage of Blenheim's Painted Red and Painted White wines. The label artwork is kept a secret, even from the staff, until shortly before the release of each vintage. These sketches are highly anticipated but are not the only pieces of art on display at Blenheim.

Blenheim also showcases artwork from the greater Charlottesville community and beyond, and in fact, much of the art on display are works by Blenheim's talented staff. The tasting room walls are lined with frequently changing shows so that visitors to Blenheim enjoy a variety of paintings, sketches, photographs, and sculptures along with great wine.

Blenheim's friendly and laid back atmosphere is due in large part to the Winemaker and General Manager, Kirsty Harmon. Kirsty has been an integral part of Blenheim's success since 2008, when Peter Matthews asked her to take over winemaking. Before coming to Blenheim, Kirsty interned at Craggy Range Winery in Hawks Bay, New Zealand. Having wanted to be a scientist from an early age, the science of making quality wine came naturally to Kirsty. In 1998, she received a degree in microbiology from the University of Virginia. It was while working as an event planner, however, that she caught the eye of wine entrepreneur Patricia Kluge, who hired Kirsty for the fledgling Kluge Estate Winery. The experience at Kluge led to a friendship with Gabriele Rausse, the father of the Virginia wine movement, whose philosophy advocates staying as true as possible to the grapes with the least amount of intervention. Kirsty further pursued her career in the wine industry by obtaining an M.S. in Viticulture and Enology from the University of California at Davis and interned internationally before her eventual return to Charlottesville, less than a mile from the vineyard where she started. If you do not see her in the tasting room you can often find her below in the barrel room or walking to the lab that she operates on the property.

© *Elizabeth Flood*

Blenheim offers a friendly and casual environment of wine and art, creating a warm, vibrant community into which all of their visitors are welcomed.

Owners/Winemakers: Reeder Family
General Manager - CJ Reeder
Vintner - Lee Reeder
Sales - Patt Reeder
Tasting Room Manager, Tours - Dawn Reeder
Year Established: 1977

Burnley Vineyards
Grape Expectations

By: Boo Barnett

Though one of the oldest Virginia wineries, small Burnley Vineyards is often overshadowed by its neighbors down the road, Barboursville and Horton. When Army Col. C.J. Reeder retired after his last posting in Charlottesville, the family decided to stay put. The Reeder family began by planting grapes in 1977 and selling their crop to other local wineries. In 1984, they took the leap to making their own wine. Col. Reeder's son Lee and his college sweetheart turned wife Dawn took over the winemaking and the tasting room. All these years later, with 32 acres currently under vine, the Reeders offer a list that runs from the venerable norton grape presentation to flavored dessert wines.

"Lots of people think wine is just like Pepsi: put in a few ingredients and boom," remarks Lee Reeder, vintner. "Really, every year is an adventure in Virginia wine." With no two harvests ever alike, Reeder relies on experience and creativity to coax the best from his vines. Every year involves careful calibrations, tweaks, new yeasts or flavoring. Every year calls for some new innovations: state of the art trimming equipment, wind machines designed to blow off frost, and deer fencing or *bear* fencing to deter the wildlife from feasting on your life's work.

Burnley produces 5,000 cases of its own wine now, with 95% of the grapes grown on their own land. You'll find Chardonnay, Cabernet Sauvignon, Norton, Barbera, Riesling, Vidal Blanc, Orange Muscat, Muscat Blanc and Chambourcin. The usual suspects are straightforward and pleasant representations: Chardonnay, Norton and Riesling, for example, remain faithful to the naked grape and are immediately identifiable to the tongue.

Dog Gone Red, Moon Mist, Aurora, and Peach Fuzz, however, require some explanation by the willing and friendly staff. All family wineries give their own special spin to each offering: otherwise, why go to the enormous bother? Burnley gives its flavored wines an extra boost; there is no mistaking the chocolate influence, the specific fruit-forward tones, or the sweet nature of the dessert wines. Whatever flavor a particular flavored wine is supposed to present, it presents big.

Many of the newest wineries build their public areas with the bridal photographer in mind. Burnley did not. The tasting room, while inviting, wastes no energy on frills and seems untouched since the early 1980s. Although there are no manicured picnic grounds, a comfortable table out back and a deck overlooking the vineyard provide quiet spots to linger with a glass of wine and enjoy the countryside. In fact, the ambience of Burnley is found not as much in the accouterments of its surroundings as in the genial nature of the Reeders themselves. The visitor will be hard pressed to find a winery with a more gracious, hospitable and engaged staff. They like having visitors so much that there is a quaint wooden A-framed house in the trees you can rent by the night.

Some have a prejudice against wineries that dabble in non-viticultural items as well; say, a line of hot sauces. The Reeders do not let this foolish narrow-mindedness interfere. This is a family business: they make what they like and they like what they make. And the wine tasting fee is a bargain ($2 for general tastings).

The affable hosts will make sure you experience the best they have to offer, and the affordable wines may just make you a repeat customer. Catch them at one of many regional tasting events or include them in a day of Barboursville area tastings.

Owners: Paul and Ruth Gorman
Winemaker: Tim Gorman
Year Established: 1985

Cardinal Point

A Wine Dream Matures in the Second Generation

By: Chris Campanelli

The Gormans' connection to Virginia wine country dates back to their purchase of property near Afton Mountain in 1985, but the dream of owning a vineyard dates to a few years before that. In the early 1970s, General Paul Gorman and his family were posted in the small city of Bad Kreuznach, Germany. This remote region of Germany is known for producing some of the world's finest Rieslings, and those few years spent in this wine-rich region were enough to instill the dream of a family vineyard for the Gormans. Upon returning to the United States, they began searching for suitable land, and eventually found an excellent site in Afton. This established a setting for the family winery, but its realization required enough patience to wait for the next generation.

When the Gormans returned from overseas, Tim Gorman was a high school student getting dragged out of bed on Saturday mornings to join his father on visits to the few existing vineyards in the region. In 1987, his dad convinced him to return home from a job in Richmond to help his architect brother John renovate the old farmhouse and tend the vines. And, as Tim tells it, "Basically, I didn't leave after that."

First as the vineyard manager and later as a winemaker, Tim adopted the Old World philosophy on the winemaking process: "the quality of the grape is the most important part of the wine." He returned to school in 1991 to study horticulture and spent ten years focused exclusively on growing excellent grapes before moving on to actual winemaking.

Meanwhile, the rest of the family had also been hard at work. While brother John was renovating, their sister Sarah was learning all she could about the wine business, and eventually took on the role of operations manager. When Tim met and later married a fellow horticulture student named Susan, she stepped right into the family business as well, serving as the tasting room manager.

The family's patience finally paid off in 2002 when they served their first vintage and opened the Cardinal Point Tasting Room. What had been a distant dream of Paul and Ruth Gorman had grown into a fully operational winery in Nelson County, Virginia.

Because the dream sprang from a personal passion rather than a career plan, the emphasis of Cardinal Point's marketing centers upon everyday enjoyment. Tim Gorman states, "My goal is to make wines that pair well with food." Such a straightforward goal is right at home in Nelson County, where pretensions and facades take a back seat to good craft and simple pleasures.

The name Cardinal Point itself keeps the operation mindful of its roots. Although spotlighting the state bird would make an appropriate name for a Virginia winery, it actually comes from a military readiness drill used by General Gorman in the late 1970s. The winery emblem is based on the four command points of the compass. From peacetime military procedure to Central Piedmont winemaking, the name is the perfect pivot point from the General's past military experience into his present winemaking venture.

The development of Cardinal Point from a couple's retirement dream to their children's daily reality is an exciting example of what's happening in Piedmont wine country today. The Gorman family shows award-winning wines, a personal aesthetic, and a family venture can blend together perfectly in Virginia.

© *Elizabeth Flood*

Owners: Claude and Genevieve DelFosse
Winemaker: Paul Mierzejewski
Year Established: 2000

Virginia has lost a pioneer: Claude DelFosse passed away on July 11, 2013, after a brief battle with cancer. Wine enthusiasts everywhere mourn his loss. Virginia was fortunate when he chose to make wine here, contributing his skill and significant expertise to fulfill Mr. Jefferson's vision.

VINEYARDS AND WINERY

DelFosse
Environmentally Sustainable Practices Make Great Wine

By: *Matt Brown*

For the active couple or family searching for a vineyard that offers more than just your standard day of wine tasting, look no further than thirty minutes south of Charlottesville in Faber, Virginia. Located in a rural community, DelFosse Vineyards is terraced into the mountains. The site offers plenty of sun, good elevation, essential wind streaming and a picturesque setting. When owners Claude and Genevieve DelFosse first came upon these 330 acres in Nelson County, it was clear that they had found something special.

The journey started in 2000 when Claude DelFosse, originally from Paris, left his career as an aeronautical engineer to start a new life as a wine maker and vineyard manager. Claude was joined in this endeavor by his wife, Genevieve DelFosse, a talented cook, local food advocate and educator with the Fairfax County School System. Over a decade later, the DelFosse family now has 22 acres under vine with plantings that include the usual Merlot, Cabernet Franc, and Petit Verdot, as well as Chambourcin, Sauvignon Blanc, Malbec, Cabernet Sauvignon, Pinot Gris, and Petit Manseng. The DelFosses have a passion for wine and have become known for their personal commitment to adopting and perfecting sustainable environmental practices for the wine world.

In the tasting room at Delfosse, winemaker Paul Mierzejewski developed a strong reputation for quality over the years. Although trained in California, he has been working in Virginia wine country since the early 1980s and has become intimately familiar with the challenges Virginia winemakers face within the industry. Through his stewardship, the grapes are allowed to display the characteristics of their terroir with the goal of ultimately producing a quality wine that embodies the unique characteristics of the region.

The grapes of DelFosse could not be in better hands and thrive in one of the only terraced vineyards in the state. Vineyard consultant Chris Hill has over 30 years of experience planting, training and managing vineyards. A celebrity in the world of Virginia wine, Chris is known for his green thumb and valuable insights. Similarly, the full time Vineyard Manager, Grayson Poats, comes to DelFosse from Wintergreen Winery with a strong background in viticulture. Along with the owners, the staff clearly enjoys creating a memorable experience for their guests.

DelFosse Vineyards hosts many events throughout the year: there are classes, and options for weekend getaways, including a century-old log cabin for rent, perched at the top of the vineyard. A popular spot for weddings and romantic weekends, this quaint little rustic cabin was renovated in 2005 and has breathtaking views overlooking the wine tasting room, lake, and terraced vineyard. It is a lovely place for guests to relax, unwind and share a bottle of wine. They also host a full events calendar of barbecues, food and wine pairing sessions, and holiday celebrations.

Claude and Genevieve DelFosse have created an inviting space for outdoor enthusiasts as well: the vineyard is home to 5.5 miles of well-kept hiking and mountain biking trails, complete with massive rocks, distinctive flora and fauna, and breathtaking views. Of course, after the hike, visitors can enjoy a picnic or wine tasting at the vineyard.

Owners: Jean and Steve Case
Winemakes: Frantz Ventre and Michael Shaps
Year Established: 2004 (Sweely Family) and
2011 (Steve and Jean Case)

EARLY
MOUNTAIN
V I N E Y A R D S

Early Mountain Vineyards
Doing Well By Doing Good

By: Boo Barnett

History, beauty, and terroir meet here in Madison, Virginia, a short drive north of Charlottesville. Named for local Revolutionary War veteran, Lt. Joseph Early, whose home served as a makeshift bed and breakfast for Revolutionary notables, this bucolic farm was made into a vineyard by the Sweely family in 2004. In 2011, Steve and Jean Case took over, planning to shake up not only a specific winery but an entire industry with their grand experiment. Their international wine tasting trips exposed them to the finest vineyards and winemakers the world over, and when they decided to create their own, they chose Virginia as a place with great potential.

Mr. Case, a co-founder and former CEO and Chairman of AOL, and Mrs. Case, the company's former Vice President for Corporate Communications, started the Case Foundation in 1997 to "encourage collaboration, support successful leaders and foster entrepreneurship," especially in underserved communities. Knowing that success can be measured in many ways other than amassing dollars, the Cases signed the Giving Pledge, the Buffet/Gates movement through which the super wealthy donate the majority of their wealth to social causes. The Cases practice their doing well by doing good philosophy in an area they love, and their push to create real stewardship for the land made for a natural interest in the former Sweely Estate Vineyard. An emphasis on good works with a superior product rather than on the owners' celebrity status keep the staff focused on creating a stellar experience for visitors.

"Early Mountain is a social enterprise—as such, all profits will go toward strengthening Virginia communities and encouraging growth, innovation...[and] learning in the Virginia wine industry. Our goal is not to make money but instead to make a difference," states Jean Case, enthusiastically.

Part of that social enterprise includes providing a showcase for all promising Virginia wines, not just their own. To that end, a visitor can sample flights that highlight themed offerings (Berries! Bright Lights and Bubbles! and Red, White and You!) from Breaux, Barboursville, Linden,

King Family, Thibaut-Janisson and others. Wine (again, their own and others) is offered also by the glass or bottle, though anyone wanting a case from a "partner winery" will need to visit that vineyard's website. Right now, their Pinot Gris and 2008 Merlot are the Early Mountain signature offerings. Selections and flight themes will change as new items are introduced. The current list, in addition to the two Early Mountain wines above, has these superior offerings: Thibaut Jannison's Blanc de Chardonnays "Monticello" and "Cuvee d'Etat," Linden's Rosé, Barboursville's Nebbiolo and "Malvaxia," and King's and Breaux' Meritages.

Of the more than 300 acres on the farm, about 38 have the slope and terroir most suitable for fine production. As the Cases plan to concentrate on the Bordeaux-style reds, they have retained Sweely's Frantz Ventre (the noted vintner from Bordeaux's Saint-Emilion) and also engaged Michael Shaps (Virginia Wineworks) and Lucie Morton (noted ampelographer and viticulturist). Sweely Vineyard, despite their careful plantings and conscientious winemaking, had flirted with foreclosure for several years before the Cases bought them out. Now, several acres of vines have been replaced and a plan to upgrade quality by a more limited cluster harvest is in force. The 2004 vines, unusually densely planted, are in their prime.

The tasting room (referred to as the Celebration Hall) is airy, open on a grand scale, with cool, chic décor. Taupe, greys and Virginia clay are the predominant colors, with heavy ceiling beams spanning the cavernous hall. Polished concrete tasting bars continue the cool feel; the entire visual experience is elegantly designed and finely coordinated. Several oversized fireplaces (indoor and out), numerous comfortable seating areas, and a variety of fire pits adorn the grounds…make sure your party knows where you are, as it would be easy to be in the same winery and never see one another! The baronial downstairs hall was made for weddings and has a patio so your party can spill out into the night.

The Market, a small food boutique in the main hall, features local cheeses, cured meats, fruits in season and assorted prepared items, heavily playing up the eat-local, drink-local theme. Picnic blankets are available for borrowing, and spending the afternoon is highly encouraged (mobile charging stations make it easy). Exceptionally family friendly, Early Mountain and its enthusiastic staff stock crayons, bubbles, board games and s'mores kits for roasting over one of their fire pits. Leashed pets are welcomed as well, with water bowls and doggie treats available. Staff members are remarkably friendly, voluble, knowledgeable and cheerful. Although this might be considered a requirement in a fledgling industry, the Early Mountain enthusiasm is a cut above. And Michelle Gueydan, with a very impressive CV despite her young age, is a marvel of charm, efficiency and effectiveness: turn her loose on your event and consider it done.

A stand-alone cottage serves as a dressing suite for brides, and at least one other outbuilding is scheduled for upgrading to the current Early Mountain standards. Though just a few minutes drive off Route 29, the views and vibe are that of a country valley.

All in all, Early Mountain is a great place to spend an afternoon with family or friends. It does not produce, by itself, a full gamut of Virginia wine, but by cleverly linking with others, it presents an upscale, relaxed and approachable introduction to Virginia's finest. With their many holiday or theme specials, Early Mountain is a great way to travel the state while seated in a most comfortable chair, enjoying a breathtaking view.

And, yes: George Washington *did* sleep here.

Owners: Heather Spiess, Bruce Spiess and
Jeffrey Miller (since December 2012)
Winemaker: Jason Hayman
Year Established: 2000

First Colony Winery

Keeping Traditions While Planning for an Exciting Future

By: Chris Campanelli

Driving down an old gravel road overhung with trees, past homes hidden behind well kept grapevines and past country dogs who greet each passerby with a friendly wag of the tail or a suspicious sneer, you are met with a beautiful rolling clearing filled with grapes. In the distance and off to the right there is a small semi-tudor style building which houses a large simple tasting room, event space, winemaking and storage facilities that encompass First Colony.

First Colony draws its name and personality from the original owner, Randolph McElroy Jr., whose family lineage can be traced all the way back to the formation of the United States, when Edmund Randolph served as George Washington's Attorney General. Randy spent the first part of his career developing and establishing a successful construction business based out of Richmond. Once the construction business stabilized, Randy's imagination returned to some of the more foundational elements of his youth, and he began to look for a way to intertwine a love of agriculture with his unique family history. As he contemplated his options in the late 1990s, the wine industry in Virginia was experiencing unprecedented growth, and the opportunity seemed like a ready-made fit for his burgeoning dream. In late 2000, Randy and his wife acquired the old Totier Creek Winery property, and First Colony Winery was established.

As a man who honors tradition, Randy began by hiring winemakers, viticulturalists, and management staff who would approach the venture in Old World French style. After the initial planting of new vines and selling the remaining Totier Creek wines, Randy hired a series of expert French winemakers who brought a European palate to bear on the development of First Colony's first vintages. This approach was quickly affirmed, as their first vintage in 2001 won over 20 awards.

First Colony uses almost exclusively French varietals grown either on their property or from within the Monticello region. They make wines from French varietals commonly successful here such as Viognier, Chardonnay, Cabernet Sauvignon, Cabernet Franc, and Merlot; they have also chosen to make blends based on less common varietals to Virginia such as Petit Manseng, Vidal Blanc and Chambourcin. As a whole, First Colony caters toward a sweeter palate, but has options available to those who prefer a variety of complex European wines.

While First Colony is in one way a bastion of tradition, in other ways it is breaking new ground in the wine community, with some of the youngest staff in the industry. Having the Richmond construction business to tend to, Randy McElroy needed to find people who could be passionately engaged and personally invested in his new endeavor. The situation proved just right for a recently graduated Virginia couple eager to find work at the intersection of hospitality and agriculture.

Beginning in 2007, Martha Hayman took over management of the tasting room, and later the general day-to-day management for First Colony Winery. In the interest of remaining near his girlfriend, Jason Hayman used his lifelong interest in plants and agriculture to secure a position as the vineyard manager the following year. Jason was intent on learning how to grow the highest quality grapes, and so used Benoit Pineau as a resource to learn everything that lies between grapes on the vine and wine in the glass. This curiosity naturally led Jason to learn the finer points of winemaking as well. When Benoit revealed that he was ready to move on to other things in 2009, Jason found himself in the unique position of being the resident expert—and with the trust of Randy McElroy and Benoit Pineau, was dubbed winemaker. It only took Jason one vintage to prove his merit, winning a gold medal for his 2009 white blend, Zephyr.

Spring forward to today and one finds Martha still managing the operations and Jason is still managing the vineyard and making the award-winning wines. The couple married in April of 2012, so the management and operation of the winery is now literally a family affair. In the VA wine culture, Martha and Jason are a case of youthful enthusiasm and excitement finding fertile ground to take root. This is something that has happened in many parts of the food industry but is only beginning to make inroads in the wine culture. Perhaps this is a sign of things to come for Virginia wine country. It is an exciting example of how the Virginia wine industry is open to any and all who are interested in making a contribution.

While First Colony still bears Randy McElroy's mark of established tradition together with young leadership, the owners have recently changed. Heather and Bruce Spiess, along with Jeffrey Miller, purchased the winery in December of 2012. By all accounts, the new owners plan to carry on the traditions that folks who frequent First Colony have come to expect. Martha is still managing the tasting room and Jason is still making the wine, while Heather's son, Austin Hamilton, has taken over management of the vineyard. The new ownership and established management team is optimistic about the future and is poised to implement some new and innovative ideas to keep First Colony a first rate Virginia winery.

Owners: Rich Evans and Lynn Davis
Winemaker: Emily Hodson
Year Established: 1999

FLYING FOX
V I N E Y A R D

Flying Fox Vineyard
A Small Family Winery Proves Less is More

By: Chris Campanelli

When Flying Fox vineyard describes itself as a "small, family-owned winery" they mean it. Planting their first vines in 1999, they keep only six and a half acres of red grapes and produce only 1,400 cases per year, which makes them perhaps the smallest operation on the Nelson County wine trail.

And when they say they want to "make the most honest wine possible from the very best grapes," they mean that, too. Their approach is to manage their vines for low yield and high fruit intensity, which emphasizes quality over quantity. In these few short years, that quality has already begun to be recognized. In just their second vintage in 2006, they won Silver, Gold, and Double Gold medals for their Cabernet Franc and Petit Verdot.

Considering their refined approach and quick success, it may come as a shock that this whole operation is a post-retirement endeavor for owners Rich Evans and Lynn Davis. Both had long careers connected to the University of Virginia hospital and academic community, and initially approached winemaking as a casual hobby. But just as the particular characteristics of the soil, climate, and weather patterns of a region lead to unique strengths in the terroir, so the particular passions and vocational experiences of Rich and Lynn have been essential in developing their own unique method of making great wines.

Rich grew up in Minnesota, where his father worked as a corn geneticist. This sparked a lifelong interest in both science and farming. Drawn initially more by the science side of that upbringing, Rich pursued a career in medicine, most of which was spent as an emergency room physician at Augusta Medical Center. Lynn also grew up in Minnesota, and got her PhD in anatomy before going on to teach biology at the University of Virginia.

This combined experience of science, biology, agriculture, and what the tasting room supervisor Carol calls Rich's "impeccable palate," makes it apparent why they adapted so easily to this highly specialized craft.

The tasting room is just off of VA route 151, commonly known as the Virginia wine trail. In colder months there's a stone hearth with a fire going on the left, and across the front is a beautiful old wooden table that spent a former life in a Nelson County general store. The walls are covered with warm-hued mountain and river paintings done by local painter Betty Arehart. With a maximum occupancy of fourteen, the setting is best described as cozy.

Guests enjoy trying all of the wines, including many award-winning ones. Flying Fox ages each of their red wines from 22 to 24 months in oak barrels. They have focused their energy on refining very typical styles for Virginia: Cabernet Franc, Merlot, Trio (a Meritage-style blend), and Petit Verdot. After savoring the taste of each of these, you might be lucky enough to try a mulled version of their Fox Red table wine, heated and enlivened with spices and honey.

Flying Fox has recently ventured into making white wines after Lynn convinced her sister Jane Ziemann and her husband John to grow vines on their property near Stuart's Draft. In January 2012, they had just bottled their first vintage of Viognier, a grape known as one of the finest fits for the Virginia terroir.

The other member of the team is already part of the fabric of Virginia wine country. Emily Hodson is the daughter of the owners of Veritas Vineyards and works side by side with Rich and Lynn. The winemaking process is housed in the Veritas facilities as the acres of Flying Fox's red wine grapes are also leased from the Veritas property. And though these are distinctly separate entities, they do have a very symbiotic relationship.

Rich and Lynn will be the first to tell you that there are many wonderful vineyards throughout Virginia. But for a unique corner of that trail where each wine is meticulously tended and served to a lucky limited few, Flying Fox has something special to offer. Judging by the quality of their wines and the passion of its owners, this is only the beginning.

Owner: Gabriele Rausse
Winemaker: Gabriele Rausse
Year Established: 1997

Gabriele Rausse Vineyards

"I have to say that I would encourage anybody to have their own little vineyard, even if they don't want to go commercial because it's a lot of fun to see what you can do with grapes." — *Gabriele Rausse.*

By: Justin Stone

Gabriele Rausse's winery sits along the same road that passes Monticello and Jefferson Vineyards as it rolls towards Albemarle's southern wine country. However, there is no dot to his winery on the Monticello Wine Trail map. There are no visible rows of cultivated grape vines to indicate his wine is being created nearby. Unlike the surrounding wineries, there is no roadside sign pointing to the tasting room because there is not one. Tucked up through the woods, along a nondescript dirt driveway reside the products and the progenitor of almost four decades of successful winemaking in Virginia. Without the presence of Gabriele Rausse the Virginia Wine Industry would not be in the state it is today, and many of the region's numerous wineries would likely not exist.

Although area wine enthusiasts are not able to visit Rausse at his winery, because it also doubles as his family's home, they are likely to see him a few miles away working the land of America's foremost wine lover as the Assistant Director of Gardens and Grounds at Monticello, a post he has had since 1995. Rausse does a bit of everything around the historic estate but his focus is on propagating the old plants and producing the 1,000 or so annual bottles of wine from the first successful vineyard at Monticello. The modern vineyard consists of over twenty varieties of European *vinifera* grapes that replicate the failed vines planted by Jefferson in 1807. It took over 170 years to overcome the agricultural plights that foiled Jefferson and for *vinifera* grape varieties to proliferate along the hills and valleys of Virginia as he had hoped. For his role in bringing this about, Rausse has been called the "Father of the modern Virginia Wine Industry."

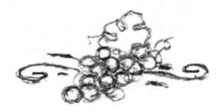

Gabriele Rausse, a native of Vicenza, Italy, arrived in the United States in early April of 1976 on an invitation from Gianni Zonin. Zonin, a friend of Rausse's father, was heir to one of the largest winemaking families in Italy who had begun their enterprise near Vicenza in the Veneto region of northern Italy over 150 years before. Rausse had previously earned his degree in Agricultural Sciences from the University of Milan, first working for the still popular Tenuta Santa Margherita winery. He had recently returned from vineyards and nurseries in Australia and Southern France when his father urged him to accompany Zonin on his ambitious venture to found a winery in the States.

Despite numerous detractors, Zonin settled on a site for the winery on a sprawling farm in the little known town of Barboursville, Virginia. At the time they were told that grapes could not be the future of Virginia, but the climate mirrored that of their native Veneto and the soil was uniquely suited to grapevines. They quickly set about planting hundreds of young *vinifera* vines from nurseries in California, among the first in Virginia since the days of Jefferson. However, the woes of Jefferson still seemed to haunt the region. Fifty percent of Barboursville's first vines died within the year. Unwilling to accept this fate, the ever affable and optimistic Rausse sought a solution that saved the nascent enterprise as Barboursville developed its own nursery where Rausse meticulously grafted their own European grape vines to American rootstocks. Grafting had already saved Europe's grape vines in the 1800's and was widely practiced on the West Coast, but his trained hands and dedicated passion perfected the practice of producing vines able to survive Virginia winters. This breakthrough opened the way for other wineries to proliferate and began Rausse's career as a preeminent viticulturist.

He stayed on at Barboursville for six years as a Manager and Vice President where he now serves on their Board of Directors. Following Barboursville, he started another nursery, vineyard, and winery near Monticello called Simeon, now known as Jefferson Vineyards. He remained there for over a decade honing his understanding of the region and what wines could be crafted from it. Then in 1994 he decided to step back from the wine industry and took the position at Monticello. It was a short reprieve. In 1997 he started his own small winery along with his then young sons, Tim and Peter. Around this time he also began experimenting with grapes from Monticello. It took a couple of years to convince Monticello to release the wine but in 1999 the first known bottles ever produced on Jefferson's grounds were sold in the gift shop. Despite aspirations to work solely at his own winery he could not resist staying at Monticello and began consulting for many of the young wineries that were beginning to thrive in the growing industry. Rausse became a respected advocate of Virginia wine and generous source of knowledge, assistance, and support to those helping build the industry.

Over the past four decades Rausse has helped found or worked directly with more then fourteen area wineries, planted over forty vineyards in the state, and countless more have benefited from his experience and dedication to developing Virginia wine regions. For many years he has been an enology instructor for the University of Virginia and Piedmont Virginia Community College. In 2011, the Virginia Agribusiness Council recognized him with the Distinguished Service Award for his service to the Virginia Wine Industry. He has also earned the Gordon W. Murchie Lifetime Achievement Award from the Virginia Wineries Association and was named Virginia Wine Person of the Year.

These illustrious awards celebrating his contributions are certainly not to be the final capstones. Rausse is still actively consulting for five area wineries and tending the grounds at Monticello. The survey ribbons hanging close to the road on his property indicate Gabriele Rausse Winery will have a tasting room to visit in the near future.

Today, Gabriele's sons Tim and Peter, who grew up surrounded by Virginia Wine, are responsible for most of the labor at the winery while Gabriele consults with them on the vineyard and wines. They grow a small amount of the grapes on their property and purchase the rest from many of the area vineyards that Gabriele helped establish. Since 1997, they have released over eighteen styles of wines but as Gabriele will attest each vintage is dependent on Virginia's fickle season. Regardless of the year, the wines he produces are gentle and smooth. They are true expressions of the grapes that he uses, and in the Italian tradition, pair beautifully with food. His Merlot, Cabernet Franc, and Pinot Gris are often found on area wine lists but his less common Nebbiolo and Pinot Noir are even more delightful. If Jefferson were around today, he and Rausse would be close friends; finding in each other a shared reverence for the region, an unwavering optimism for its future, and an enjoyment of fine wines.

Owners: Jeff and Michelle Sanders
Winemaker: Michael McFarland
Year Established: 2006

Glass House Winery
Exquisite Setting, Wine, and Chocolate

By: Boo Barnett

Imagine the gentle sway of palm trees, the scent of tropical blooms and your own private table set with artisan chocolates and a flight of local wines. Now, imagine that you are still in Albemarle County, a short ride from Charlottesville. A fantasy? Yes, but one brought to life by the enterprising team of Jeff and Michelle Sanders, who welcome you to their world of wine and chocolate in bucolic Free Union.

When the Sanders decided to leave their home on the remote Honduran island of Roatan, their goals were clear: excellent education for their children, a welcoming community, and a beautiful setting in which to establish their dream vineyard. An exhaustive search took them to the renowned viticulture regions of the world, all of which honed their vision for the perfect winery. It was on a solo trip to Charlottesville, however, that Jeff phoned Michelle to announce, "Honey, I found it – we're home!"

And home they have been, since 2006, with a geothermally conditioned glass house for tropical plants, a thriving vineyard and a swoon-worthy line of artisan chocolates. Tidy, trimmed rows of Viognier, Chambourcin and Barbera vines promise a luscious future, with 12 acres under cultivation. These varietals are noted for making the most of the local terroir, an aspect of careful stewardship so prized by the Sanders. Though much of their wine is from these estate grown grapes, this young vineyard can turn to more mature ones as a source for additional varietals.

The Glass House Caribbean vibe begins with bright sculptures and eye-catching yard art, pointing the way to the tasting room. There, the charming maître' d, Dogbert, sets the tone. They may be serious about their wines here, but they are also serious about simple family pleasures, and having a cheerful hound at the door starts the tasting with a laugh. "He's the most petted dog in Albemarle County," smiles Michelle.

The tasting room itself is an inviting example of clean, green architecture: thoughtful lighting, a beautiful wood bar and niches crafted to showcase Glass House offerings. Go left, and a beautiful deck overlooking the pond provides splendid seating on warm days. Go right and fall under the spell of the tropical palm house. Either way, as you enter, one of the bright, knowledgeable staff is sure to call out a cheerful greeting.

A sample tasting covers their Viognier, Pinot Gris and Vino Signora whites and moves onto their 21st (a Governor's Cup medalist), C-Villian, and Barbera reds. The owners' lighthearted tone rings through his description of the lightning-surviving Pinot Gris vines, saying they are "infused with healing powers...when taken in the proper dosage, of course." Last, and certainly not least (judging by crowd reaction), is the mysterious Meglio del Sesso and a sampling of a chocolate, a bewitching combination. Rich Chambourcin and Cabernet Franc are blended with ground dark chocolate, creating a dessert wine that justifies the smoldering eyes painted on the label. The tasting notes tease the guest to ask for a translation, and to judge whether it lives up to its name!

Jeff, who is as comfortable chatting about geothermal heating ponds and propagation techniques for tropical fruit trees as he is about wines, is enthusiastic about his and Michelle's shared vision of Virginia viticulture.

"There is tremendous energy in the Virginia wine world, and really special things [are] happening. Here, all the winemakers have each other's best interests at heart – if it is good for your vineyard, it is good for Virginia wine, and therefore good for everybody. The cooperation and lack of competition is pretty much unheard of in other wine making regions." Having Brad McCarthy as a consultant early on also served to undergird their enthusiasm, who claims that "Virginia wine improves, every year!"

This camaraderie seems to suit the Sanders perfectly. After all, how many other vineyards throw a Polynesian pit pork luau, complete with music under the palms? They have many special events lined up, with a full calendar of local musicians and entertainers on the website calendar. Jeff offers special learning opportunities for patrons who wish to learn winemaking and blending, and gives special cellar and vineyard tours that provide more depth than is available on a simple guided walk.

Glass House chocolates alone would make the beautiful ride to Free Union worthwhile. Their greenhouse fruits and flavors inspire Michelle's line of handcrafted delights. Pineapples (the Southern symbol for hospitality) not only show up as architectural motifs here; they actually grow in the greenhouse. Coffee beans (grown in the glass house), and their estate wines also find their way into the delicious chocolates, which are available individually or in attractive boxes. Flavors include a delectable salted caramel, Red Wine Cream, an Earl Grey, and an espresso-Kahlua. It may be too hard to choose, so treat yourself to one of each!

And, of course, the Glass House winery corks its bottles with an elegant glass seal. Not only do they fit the theme perfectly, these seals also make opening easy and storage airtight.

At the end of a recent tasting, guests lingered under the bananas, nursing the final tantalizing drops of the Meglio after a picnic. Faint strains of music drifted by and children played an impromptu game of tag in the jungle. Dogbert wandered from table to table, the perfect host on a perfect day, all part of a vision that Jeff and Michelle Sanders built from the ground up.

Owner: John Grace
Winemaker: Jake Busching
Year Established: 2013

Grace Estate Winery
Old Vines Create Graceful Traditions

By: Boo Barnett

John Grace fell in love, and he fell hard. Impossible to blame him- everyone who visits Ireland and is lucky enough to visit the Mount Juliet resort feels the same. Add to that the discovery that some of his ancestors had once owned part of that venerable estate, and it was an unquenchable passion. Small wonder, then, that when he stumbled across the lovely Mount Juliet estate in bucolic Crozet, its purchase was a foregone conclusion. The magnificent house was based on the Irish original, and its rolling green hills were possibly even more verdant, more alluring than those on the Emerald Isle. And, there were the grapes…

Mount Juliet had been selling its high quality grapes to other vintners since 1999. When the Grace family made the decision to establish its own winery, it was imperative that they find someone whose vision and taste would match their own. As they reside in Switzerland most of the year, the Graces needed a trusted resident expert whose experience with all aspects of the business could be relied upon to carry it forward independently.

Fortunately for the wine lovers of the Monticello AVA, the Grace Estate at Mount Juliet Farm went long for talent and secured the renowned Jake Busching (the wunderkind formerly of Pollak, Jefferson and Keswick Vineyards). This self styled "winegrower" takes the Old World holistic approach of being both the farmer and the vintner: after all, who knows the grape and its potential better than the ones who nurture it?

Jake Busching is all about the soil- as any farmer knows (and he grew up farming in Minnesota), the terroir is what makes each fruit or wine or bacon slice really sing in the local vernacular. Keeping that flavor real, and local, is why their wines are all made with their own grapes, which include Viognier, Chardonnay, Petit Manseng, Petit Verdot, Merlot, Cab Franc, Cab Sauvignon, Malbec and Tannat. With 65 acres now under vine, and a 550 acre estate to expand, maintain and perfect, Busching keeps enough fruit to make several thousand cases of the Grace Estate's own wines, reserving the remainder for other Monticello Appellation wineries. As an active member of several local wine associations, Busching is committed to expanding the possibilities of our local agribusiness and agritourism.

Having a string of awards to his own credit might satisfy many, but Busching's pet collaborative wine project "3" brings in Veritas' Emily Pelton and King Family's Matthieu Finot, each of whom contributes a select variety to mix with the others. This spirit of friends and peers joining in with the best of a year's harvest in such a collegial manner exemplifies the state of Virginia's wine industry: purposeful but interdependent. Every vintner interviewed remarked that the industry was only as good as the last glass any visitor tried, and that the best competition was based on knowledge, cooperation and collaboration.

The approach to the tasting room at Grace is a long, quiet hum through fields and fields of vines. Brief glimpses of the house, long panoramic views of the Blue Ridge and those rolling acres of vines make the ride a perfect component of the experience: Slow down. Enjoy. Appreciate.

The cheerful staff, though few in number, enthusiastically welcome visitors to "Our Barnery," a nickname that seems to sum up their serious but unpretentious approach to wine. Tasting room hostess Caitlin Andrus noted that their small converted hay barn reflects an understated approach, but it is understated in the same way Old World monastery is: clean, well edited and simply made from the purest ingredients. Even the barrel room was a model of thoughtfully arranged, beautifully placed items with not one extraneous thing. Andrus also pointed out the unexpected, very Zen silo off the tasting room. There, three plain benches provide seating in the still, unadorned, circular room open to the sky. After seeing it, any winery without one seems, well… incomplete. Another silo on the property will be used in a similar fashion, and Andrus hinted of a future Silo Society Wine Club.

A day at Grace is a visit with a gracious, self-confident, stunningly beautiful and worldly friend, a friend who is still young at heart and who knows the value of the quiet moment of contemplation. Who could blame John Grace for falling in love? We fell, too.

Owner: Dennis Horton
Winemaker: Mike Heny
Year Established: 1988

Horton Vineyards

A Rhône Rogue in the East

By: *Justin Stone*

From his small farm established in 1983, Dennis Horton, proprietor and original winemaker of Horton Vineyards, became a pioneer of Virginia wine. Among the largest producers in the state today, the European-style winery includes a stone tower, spiral staircase, and vast chambered barrel room. The fifty-five acre estate is one of three sites where Horton grows French, Italian, Eastern European and native grape varietals. Dennis realized the warm Virginia summers ripen almost any grape variety, but the humidity of the region favors grapes with thick skins and loose clusters. He scoured the world for varietals that flourish in Virginia and made many discoveries, two of which stand out in the history of Virginia wine: the rise of Rhône Valley wines and the revival of the Norton grape in its birth state.

Dennis began planting vines at Horton in 1988. Experience as an amateur viticulturist told him varietals such as Cabernet Franc were well suited for Virginia. In 1991, he was among the first to produce a Cabernet Franc on a commercial scale. Dennis understood what humid and often stormy Virginia summers do to delicate late-ripening grapes such as Cabernet Sauvignon that grow well in California. California, the greenhouse for American wines with names like Mondavi and Kistler steered the American palate toward full-bodied, richly aromatized Cabernets and Chardonnays. Throughout the second half of the last century, these classic varietals migrated to other wine regions, including Virginia, with varied degrees of success. Virginia has a great vintage of Cabernet Sauvignon 1 out of every 8 years, while California consistently make reserves from each vintage. Before this distinction was widely known, Dennis started taking his cues from a progressive group of California winemakers, dubbed the Rhône Rangers.

In the 1980s, the Rhône Rangers promoted varietals from the famous Rhône Valley region in southern France where notoriously hot summers and steep granite slopes enrich varietals such as Marsanne, Rousanne, Viognier, Syrah, and Grenache with naturally thick skins and loose clusters. During a trip to the Rhône, Dennis experienced these wines first hand and understood their potential for Virginia. Planting these grapes at Horton initially brought skepticism because they were unfamiliar to the region. Dennis became the "Lone Rhône Ranger of the East." His audacity paid off when Horton's second vintage of Viognier was awarded a 91 out of 100 by the prominent American wine critic Robert Parker. The burgeoning industry took note. Today you can hardly find a wine flight in Virginia that does not include a Viognier.

Horton Vineyards became a laboratory for varietals that few dared to grow in Virginia or, in the case of the Norton grape, had not been seen in over six decades. No one knows the true origin of the Norton grape. Its name comes from Dr. Daniel Norton, who claims to have stumbled across the vitis vinifera (European) and *vitis aestivalis* (American) hybrid in his garden in the 1820s. Norton foresaw that the dark inky wine made from the grape had a destiny beyond his Magnolia Farm. Unfortunately, his death in 1842 prevented him from seeing the Norton reach its height of national and international acclaim. In 1861, a claim by F.W. Lemosy that his father found the grape growing wild on an island in the James River and subsequently sold cuttings to Dr. Norton tarnished the doctor's legacy posthumously but added mystery and intrigue to the grape as it Rosé to prominence.

By the 1850s, the Norton grape spread to Pennsylvania, the Ohio River Valley, and Missouri. There, it won over German immigrants who are credited with widely popularizing it, most notably at Stone Hill Winery in Hermann, Missouri. In 1873, an American Norton was voted "best red wine of all nations" at the Universal Exhibition in Vienna, Austria. At the turn of the century the Norton looked as if it would be the grape to finally place American wine on the map but with the passage of the 18th Amendment, prohibition effectively pushed varietals like the Norton to the brink of extinction.

Dennis knew the story of the Norton. He grew up in Hermann, Missouri near Stone Hill Winery. Moreover, he believed the Norton was, "a grape that originated [in

Virginia], a strong, disease-resistant grape, a good grape, that went all the way from here to Cincinnati, and then all the way from there to Missouri." Born in Virginia soil, Horton resolved to bring it home again.

In 1988, Dennis contacted Stone Hill Winery seeking norton vines and soon after planted the first norton grapevines in Virginia since the repeal of prohibition. Now seen as his greatest act as a purveyor of Virginia varietals, today more than twenty-five Virginia wineries make wine from Norton grapes. Although it remains a little-known varietal for the majority of consumers in the region, Dennis believes it will once again win over wine enthusiasts.

Dennis now entrusts the primary winemaking responsibilities to his long-time assistant, Mike Heny. Virginia continues to evolve as a wine-producing region and is only just beginning to explore the many well-suited grape varietals, thanks in large part to Dennis Horton. With a youthful exuberance, he acknowledges the significant contributions he made to the Virginia wine industry, but tempers such acclaim with the adage, "[It's] better to be lucky than smart." Perhaps a small part of the success at Horton Vineyards is due to luck, but the passion, originality, and savviness of Dennis Horton has unquestionably contributed to the greater quest for quality and diversity in Virginia wine.

Owners: Stanley and Svaha Woodward
Winemaker: Chris Ritzcovan
Year Established: 1981

Jefferson Vineyards

Fulfilling Jefferson's Dream

By: Justin Stone

It has been over two hundred and fifty years since Jefferson walked the property that is home to Jefferson Vineyards today. The winery bears his name and produces wines from vines planted on his former land. Even though Jefferson Vineyards has no current official link to the Sage of Monticello, the winery's history is intertwined with his legacy as America's first distinguished wine enthusiast.

The vineyard is located on six hundred acres of beautiful, rolling hills beneath the ridges that rise to the doorsteps of Monticello and Ash Lawn. The land was surveyed by the early settlers of Colonial America, and the winery continues to respect and embrace their place in this heritage.

In 1773, Philip Mazzei sailed to Virginia from London, where he had been a distinguished wine seller. He was a Florentine Renaissance Man, experienced as a merchant, surgeon, and horticulturist who, through business dealings (likely wine sales), had befriended the American polymath Thomas Jefferson. Jefferson, eager to have a kindred intellectual and wine enthusiast nearby, deeded one hundred ninety three acres just south east of Monticello to Mazzei. Among Mazzei's first acts as a Virginia landowner was naming the property Colle, French for "hill," and planting vinifera grape vines. Like Jefferson, he never saw his dream of producing a Virginia wine come to fruition. Soon after he established the Colle vineyard, Jefferson and Madison persuaded Mazzei to aid the American Revolution, and he left his young estate in 1778 to seek foreign investments for his adopted country. Upon his return in 1783 he found the grounds and vines ruined by the war. Dejected by the failure of his vineyard and dissatisfied with the post-Revolutionary political climate, Mazzei left Virginia in 1785. Although the Colle estate later expanded to over eight hundred acres of sprawling hills and stayed in the family through the turn of the century, Mazzei never returned.

The estate passed through various hands and uses over the next 150 years, at times supporting herds of livestock or rows of fruit trees. In 1939 Stanley Woodward purchased the property, and it has stayed with his family since. As the Virginia wine industry began to blossom, the Woodwards hoped to re-establish grapes on the land and accomplish what its previous owners had not—making fine Virginia wine. In the late 1970s Gabriele Rausse helped plant the vines in one of his first post-Barboursville ventures. Often called the "father of the Virginia wine industry," Rausse went on to establish many of the wineries located in the Monticello AVA. Within a few years, Jefferson Vineyards had their first vintage and a thriving business.

Two hundred years prior, Philip Mazzei had believed that Virginia's soil and climate were better suited than any other for the production of wine. Jefferson Vineyards was among the first group of wineries to prove that, despite earlier failings, Virginia could produce outstanding wines from native and European vines. Today, Jefferson is known for its Reserve Chardonnay, Cabernet Franc, and Meritage. As fitting tributes to their heritage, their prized wines bear the signature of the estate's first owner.

When visiting Jefferson Vineyards, the unassuming connection to history surrounds you. A Virginia historical marker about Colle stands at the vineyard's entrance and visitors are offered a historical tour by one of the seasoned staff. An old, faded green farmhouse with a wrap-around porch functions as the office, giving a sense of old-fashioned country hospitality to the vineyard.

The tasting room has the appearance of a converted row barn, which fits in with the other grange buildings and history of farming on the estate. Owner Stanley Woodward's painting of Don Juan, the patron rooster of the property, adorns a wall in the tasting room along with the bottles of Vin Rouge. Don Juan III or perhaps even Don Juan IV now presides over the vineyard.

Jefferson is a beautiful and historically significant spot in the heart of the Monticello AVA, and was among the early wineries to re-establish Virginia as a premier wine-producing region. Through their vineyard and wines they remind us of Virginia's history as the first grape-growing state in America, one of Thomas Jefferson's dearest desires.

Owner: Al and Cindy Shornberg
Winemaker: Stephen Barnard
Year Established: 1999

Keswick Vineyards
Making Great Wine in a Grand Setting

By: Justin Stone

When Al and Cindy Schornberg moved from the Detroit area to the historic four hundred-acre Edgewood Estate near Keswick Virginia, they took a step back into history. Considered to be the "western frontier" during the Colonial period, the rolling hills and rich lands of the Keswick area were sought after for their rich soil, temperate climate and accessible location. The area was a primary route between the growing city of Charlottesville and the capitals in the East – first Williamsburg and later Richmond. The Schornbergs had not just settled on land rich in history, they had also stepped back into their family's heritage. Two generations earlier, the family had owned Messena Cellars in France. Al still recalls his grandfather's stories of working in the family's vineyards. In 1999, Al and Cindy left the high tech corporate world for the pastoral lifestyle where Al had always dreamed of indulging his love of viticulture. "I just wanted to be able to enjoy a really good wine that I made. There's something very natural and satisfying about that." Keswick Vineyards was born from this desire.

After six years of intense searching, the Schornbergs decided on the Keswick estate because of its place in the burgeoning Virginia wine region, its nutrient rich and variant soil, and the grand residence on the property. The present Edgewood Estate was originally part of an 18,000-acre royal grant to Nicholas Meriwether in 1727, which became the Castle Hill estate. Today, much of that tract has been parceled into smaller estates like Edgewood with the largest tract still home to the current Castle Hill. In 1911, George Barclay Rives constructed the elegant home at Edgewood that the Schornbergs purchased in 2010. Rives was a direct descendent of Meriwether, and to pay homage to their estate's history, Keswick produces a Rives Red each year under a signature label.

Since they first planted vines in 2000, the Schornbergs have carefully stewarded the rich soil and sloping terrain to produce wines characteristic of the area. Neighboring Horton Vineyards had shown what produced well in this region, so the Schornbergs introduced a diverse array of three-year old vines that included Viognier, Chardonnay, Merlot, Malbec, Cabernet Franc, Chambourcin, Petite Verdot and Norton. While they have maintained many of these varietals, others have been added subsequently. Their first vintage, the 2002 Viognier Reserve, received national recognition, as it does today. In contrast, since planting, their Malbec has produced only a single vintage. As a result, during the 2011 winter they pulled every vine of Malbec in favor of varietals that are better suited to Virginia. Natural order is still respected by skilled viticulturists and vintners.

The distinguished winemaker behind Keswick Vincyard's wines is Stephen Barnard, who has been making award-winning wine in Virginia for over a decade. A native of South Africa, Stephen's introduction to wine came from Groot Constantia Winery, the oldest winery in South Africa. It was there that Stephen began pouring and leading tours before transitioning into the cellar and earning his appointment as assistant winemaker. After earning his enology degree he moved on to the well-known Flagstone winery where he trained exclusively in reds. An Ohio State internship program led to opportunities to work for American wineries. He had his choice of placement, among the great viticultural regions on the West Coast, and while Stephen had not placed Virginia among his top choices, his advisors urged him to consider the nascent region. In 2000, just as Al and Cindy were beginning Keswick, they were introduced to the young winemaker and invited him to join them on their estate. With this unique opportunity and challenge, he thought he could learn more in a year here than in California. After more than a decade of vintages he is still intrigued.

"Virginia is a vintage state," he says. Consistency in wine is a desirable characteristic: winemakers and customers alike look for it as it is synonymous with proven, identifiable qualities. But here, the wines are governed by the variant range and uncertain conditions that come with each growing season. According to Stephen, "The only consistency [in Virginia] is that every year is different." This challenges winemakers every year to adapt their processes in order to produce wines that retain their signature character. As a testament to Stephen's skills as a winemaker, Keswick continues to win awards each year for their Viognier and reserve reds. Today, Al and Cindy's faith in him is unwavering, but this was not always the case.

When Stephen first arrived at Keswick he accepted room and board in an efficiency apartment the Schornbergs had created above the winery and tasting room. Katherine, one of the Schornbergs' six children, began keeping the apartment stocked with the comforts of home. A friendship formed between the young winemaker and the proprietors' daughter, a friendship that led to a courtship and then to what Stephen jovially refers to as, "job security." However, prior to marrying Katherine and officially joining the Schornberg family, Stephen was released as Keswick's winemaker. He went to work at Rappahannock Winery for two vintages. While at Rappahannock, his 2005 Viognier won Virginia's Governor's Cup for Best White Wine. That year Rappahannock's grapes had been purchased from Keswick. Al was convinced Stephen belonged at Keswick and asked him to resume making their wines, to the delight of Cindy and Katherine.

Stephen says he began making wines as a means to travel the world, and despite settling in Virginia for the past decade he hasn't lost his intrepid spirit. He continues to push forward and enjoy the lessons learned at Keswick.

Keswick Vineyards has proven they can consistently make excellent wines that reflect the area by pushing themselves to anticipate and respond to each variant season. This has allowed them to remain at the forefront of the evolving landscape of the Virginia wine industry and given credence to their belief that they stand among the top wineries in the state.

Owners/Winemakers: Bob and Doriene Steeves
Year Established: 1994

Kilaurwen Winery
An Irish Lilt in the Foothills

By: Boo Barnett

Located 8 miles from the Swift Run Gap entrance to the breathtaking Shenandoah National Park, Kilaurwen Vineyards is a small, family vineyard in the old-fashioned sense. Established in 1994, the Steeves family began supplying grapes for other vintners in the Monticello region. By 2009, they decided to keep some of those award-winning grapes and make their own family brand.

Bob Steeves grew up in a farm family, and took a pharmacy degree from the University of Connecticut. He and his wife Doriene, a self-described "Army brat" from all over, considered a number of alternatives to make their current farm into a viable business. When family friends in Northern Virginia invited them to come pick grapes at a small vineyard, a vision began to emerge. What a perfect way to combine scientific education, love of rural land and a strong desire for a venture the entire family could join!

Very laid back, Kilaurwen seeks to be neither the high-turnover industrial vineyard, nor the artfully designed bridal magazine backdrop. Their motto is "We are in the wine business for the wine, not for the business." Bring your own picnic and blanket, settle down to admire the timeless

360-degree views and prepare for a quiet, country experience. The tasting room is not fancy, but with views like theirs, why waste a moment indoors?

Their location, a south-facing slope in the foothills of the Blue Ridge, provides a steady airflow that is an essential aid in combating mildew during Virginia's muggy late summer. Ten acres of vinifera grapes is all they grow and all they wish to grow—the goal is to be the best, not the biggest. Unusual for this area, five acres are in Riesling, which is a vineyard favorite.

They seek to make a few really enjoyable offerings for family and friends (which includes you) and to stay small and personal. Cab Franc takes pride of place here, having just won the silver medal at the 2012 Southeast Wine Competition. Their Fiesta White won silver there as well, and their Riesling was chosen for the 2011 Wine Bloggers' Convention.

The Steeves take their Kilaurwen show on the road often, attending a wide variety of events and festivals, so check their website before visiting. They also host events at the vineyard, bringing in bands and entertainment for the enjoyment of picnicking wine tasters.

As for the name, what could be more "family business" than combing the names of your children for the business moniker? Kimberlee, Laura and Wendy, thus immortalized, see their names on the vineyard banners, playfully spelled out in shamrock green Celtic lettering. Theirs is an intergenerational family business, too, with an age range of young teens to septuagenarians.

A family member is always within shouting distance, should you have a question or need another bottle. Kilaurwen also actively solicits volunteer participation at festivals and throws in a free Kilaurwen t-shirt as an additional reward. A post card setting, a welcoming family doing what they love and award-winning wines all add up to a lovely autumn afternoon.

Winemaker: Matthieu Finot
Owners: David & Ellen King, Carrington King, Stuart
King, and James King
Year Established: 1998

King Family Vineyards
Fate Leads to Virginia Wine Royalty

By: Bit Pressley

When David and Ellen King moved to Crozet, Virginia from Texas and purchased Roséland Farm in 1996, starting a vineyard on the 327-acre farm was the last thing on their minds. They fully intended to concentrate on their horses and the alfalfa crop that was already in production. Fate, however, as is often the case, had it's own design in the form of a visit from a stranger who put the vineyard bug in their ear. He suggested that the terroir of the property was ideal for growing grapes. And thus a stranger's suggestion led to the creation a vineyard destined to become royalty within the Virginia wine industry.

The first eight acres of King Family Vineyards were designed and planted beginning in 1998. The Kings hired Chris Hill, a well know vineyard consultant, to recommend planting sites and the best grape varietals in the region. By 2000 they produced their first vintage of only 500 cases with winemaking consultant Michael Shaps. Today, King Family Vineyards produces over 7,000 cases of wine and has 30 acres under vine. The varietals planted include Chardonnay, Merlot, Cabernet Franc, Petit Verdot, Petit Manseng and Malbec. The farm is also home to a protected waterfowl preserve and the land is under conservation easement with the Virginia Outdoor Foundation.

The name King Family is certainly appropriate, as all of the family is involved in the venture. The King's eldest son, Carrington, obtained a horticulture degree with an emphasis on fruit production at the University of Maryland. Carrington and his brother Stuart manage the vineyards and can also be found in the cellar or helping with the bottling. The King's youngest son, James, is a United States Marine Corps veteran and recently joined the family business as the Tasting Room Manager.

In 2006, the Kings decided a full time winemaker was needed so they hired Matthieu Finot, who hails from Crozes, in the Rhône Valley of France, and has broad experience in wine making not only in France, but in Italy and South Africa as well. Matthieu has a healthy respect for the Old World style of winemaking, as well as the innovative cutting edge of the New World. The King Family also works with local sparkling wine expert, Claude Thibaut, to produce a sparkling blanc-de-blanc brut. Mr. Thibaut, a fourth generation Champagne producer, hailing from the Champagne region of France, has incredible skill in the production of sparkling wines using the traditional méthode champenoise.

King Family Vineyards is well known for its Meritage, a Bordeaux-style blend of four red varietals. Other popular wines include Crosé, a Provence-style rosé, and "7", a port style wine crafted from Merlot and aged in Woodford Reserve Kentucky Bourbon barrels. In addition, the winery also produces a Chardonnay-Viognier blend called "Roséland", a single varietal Chardonnay and Viognier, as well as Viognier, Merlot, Cabernet Franc and Petit Verdot. To round out the portfolio, a desert wine called "Loreley" is made from Viognier and Petit Manseng grapes.

The Tasting Room and grounds of King Family

Vineyards are open year round. Outdoor seating is available on two expansive patios where visitors enjoy great wine coupled with breathtaking vistas of the Blue Ridge Mountains. In cooler months, the Tasting Room welcomes visitors with a warm fire in the stone fireplace. The grounds are also home to The Carriage House, an event space, available for private celebrations of all kinds. The North Gallery of the Carriage House showcases the work of local artists. King Family Vineyards also hosts weekly polo matches, held on Sundays from Memorial Day through early October. Guests are welcome to watch from the patio or can tailgate to be closer to the action. Spectators are encouraged to call the vineyard for match updates.

During the summer months, King Family Vineyards hosts "First Wednesdays" when the tasting room hours are extended until 8:30pm giving visitors the opportunity to come by and enjoy their favorite wine while watching the sun sink down into the Blue Ridge. As always, visitors can purchase artisanal meats and cheeses from the Tasting Room or bring their own picnic.

Fate brought the King family together to create a tremendously successful business; one that is an integral part of the Virginia wine industry. Each member of the King family has worked hard to build and maintain a reputation for having quality wines and a top-notch staff who understand hospitality. Any trip to the Monticello Wine Trail area would be incomplete without a visit to the King Family Vineyards!

Owners: Ed and Janet Puckett
Winemaker: Riann Rossouw
Year Established: 2006

Lovingston Winery
The Secret is Out

By: Matt Brown

Can you keep a secret? Lovingston is a hidden gem on the Monticello Wine Trail. Tucked away into the foothills of the Blue Ridge Mountains about 35 miles south of Charlottesville, Lovingston Winery is a small, family-run boutique winery which produces wine from traditional French varieties, as well as several hybrids. Their densely planted, 8.5-acre vineyard on Josie's Knoll is divided between Merlot, Cabernet Franc, Petit Verdot, Pinotage, Chardonnay, and Seyval Blanc. Vineyard Manager/Owner Ed Puckett, along with South African Winemaker Riann Rossouw, produces small batch, high quality wines which are expressive of the local terroir and Riann's unique style. Formerly from Oakencroft Vineyards, Riann brings with him years of experience, South African roots, and a personal twist. The owner's daughter, Stephanie, acts as Riann's assistant—doing her part in supporting the family business. Stephanie and her father, Ed, are both graduates of the University of Virginia. Although the family originally grew grapes in Georgia, the love for central Virginia instilled in them by the University, as well as a desire to produce higher quality wine grapes, drew them back to the Charlottesville area.

One interesting feature of the winery is their integration of "gravity flow." This setup allows for gravity to do most of the work with moving the grape clusters and wine from processing, into the tanks/barrels, and into bottles. This more gentle method helps limit the extraction of harsh phenolic compounds that can make the wine unpleasant. This method is used to some degree throughout the world of wine making, however, it is a very rare technique within the Commonwealth as it can be expensive to build such a winery and a certain terrain is needed (gravity flow wineryies are typically built into hillsides). Luckily the terrain at Lovingston is well suited to this practice.

Starting in the vineyard, nearly everything is done by hand. During the growing season vines and their canopies are closely maintained through a process called devigoration—the removal of the green growth such as leaves in order to force the vine to focus more on the fruit and less on the leaves. Also, many of the grape clusters will be cut off the vine early on, so each vine can concentrate on fewer clusters. Lovingston is acutely aware that a lower yield produces a higher quality, thus they have planted their vines about twice as densely as is typical (1200 vines/acre) and have used a high trellising system (about 10 feet tall) in order to allow the leaves the most exposure to sun as is possible.

This exposure allows the processes of photosynthesis and transpiration to occur, which increases the sugar and ripeness in the individual grapes, giving them the qualities they need to produce world-class wines.

Harvest is also carried out by hand using a team of vineyard workers who hand pick each cluster of grapes. While the white grapes are pressed as whole clusters (as is traditional), the red grapes are de-stemmed before being pressed. The family believes this additional step produces cleaner, more balanced red wines. The owners, their daughter, and their winemaker then sort through the fruit as gravity carries it into stainless steel tanks for maceration—the process by which color and tannin is extracted from the skins and seeds of red grapes. Once this process is complete, the Pucketts age most of the volume of the red wines in oak, producing smooth and age-worthy red wines.

Many of Lovingston's offerings are under $20 a bottle and they offer some of the best values in VA wine, especially considering that their production is so low—around 2000 cases a year. Although the winery produces a number of exciting white wines, Winemaker Riann has earned a strong reputation for his impressive red wines including his Merlot, Pinotage, and Chambourcin. He also produces his own private label, named "r", which is a very small production Merlot. In December of 2011, Lovingston's "Josie's Knoll Estate Reserve" received a score of 89 from Wine Enthusiast magazine. This was a big honor to Ed, Riann, and the entire team at Lovingston.

On many trips to Lovingston, you'll encounter most, if not all, of the family. As such a small production winery, each member of the family is on site, working overtime, year-round, to continue producing their quality wines.

Owners/Winemakers: Barry and Ellen Moss
Year Established: 2012

Moss Vineyards

Elegant Architecture, Stunning Views and Stellar Wine

By: Boo Barnett

Even in an area known for its breathtaking views, Moss Winery is notable for its spectacular location. 1000 feet up and swept by rising thermals and plunging downdrafts, the circular and katabatic wind patterns make the surrounding forests roar. That, and granite rich soil, ensure the vines that survive have the toughness required to create the best wines. And survive they do, for which fans of the Cabernet Sauvignon, Petit Verdot, Viognier, Varmentino and Merlot grapes can be very grateful.

When you sit on the terrace overlooking the rumpled Blue Ridge, it all seems inevitable: the unforgettable scenery, the delectable wine, the crisply modern tasting room and headquarters. Twin freestanding chimneys flank the glass walled winery, paying tribute to that most heart tugging of Appalachian totems: the abandoned stone fireplace, lonesome and crumbling in the woods. But before the first vines were planted in 2007, this was a heavily wooded, uninhabited mountain, so rugged that real estate agents were reluctant to show it. When Barry and Ellen Moss made it to the current tasting room site, a friend climbed one of the tallest pines and snapped a cellphone photo of the valley below, as they could only guess what vistas would be revealed by clearing. Now, it seems, their intuition has paid off.

It had been during a family vacation in Italy, enjoying the rich leisure that comes from long dinners of regional specialties and local wines savored on a Mediterranean patio, that the Mosses looked at one another and thought, "We want this, at home." Though a Californian by birth, Ellen agreed with her Virginian husband that staying close to his family was paramount. Then, focused tastings of what was currently produced convinced them that "Virginia wine" was not an oxymoron. Teaming up with some of the finest and most knowledgeable tastemakers, vintners and wine experts, the Mosses searched for the right place, knowing that the specific microclimates and soil composition would tell them which grapes to cultivate. Then they spotted a rutted road that hair pinned off a rural lane in tiny, forgotten Nortonsville and began their labor of love.

When that phrase is used about vineyards, it often means more love than labor. Not so at Moss. Barry, a noted architect, and Ellen, an urban planning and IT professional, decided to "keep our day jobs" and commute every weekend to this remote corner of Albemarle County. After a long predawn trek from Norfolk on Saturday mornings, they would roll out of the car and toil until dark. A brief overnight stay, another long day of boulders and digging and planting, and then back through the night to Norfolk and the clean, quiet professional offices where they could dream of vines and vintages during the week.

They worked hard, and they worked smart. By getting the most experienced and well-regarded names in the business, they avoided costly missteps. Two of the go-to experts whose influences are so evident in the Moss wines are Gabriele Rausse, whose work laid the foundations for all fine Virginia vineyards, and Luca Paschina, the Zonin's excellent vintner at Barboursville. Their Old World Italian approach married seamlessly with the elegant simplicity of the Moss family aesthetic.

The 5000 vines on site are supplemented by Cab Franc and Barbera grapes, which are purchased off vineyard (a common local practice). New vines are going in, all arranged with the perfect orientation for their site, and established vines are rigorously tended. Consultations with those same experts, who are now dear friends as well as collaborators, continue as they all search for the perfect blends to make the most of what each wildly individual harvest throws at them.

The Mosses seem genuinely interested in a visitor's impressions of a given wine. When asked for their own in-house favorites, well, the answer may change by the day or the hour. Their Arquitectonica, for example, has already been heralded for its unusually fine aging potential- good now, yes, but it's going to be something quite memorable if only you can keep your hands off it for a few years. The Vino Rosso, however, is a toothsome blend for drinking now, and the dry Rosé has already been dubbed the perfect summer pool wine. Oh, and then there's...

"And that's one of the many marvelous things about a small, boutique winery," Ellen enthused. "You get to taste it all!" Keeping in mind Galileo's summation that "wine is sunlight, held together by water," Moss Vineyards has captured all sorts of days for its visitors to enjoy, sip by sip. The dramatic scenery (just look at the website photos!), the beautifully crafted architecture, the tastefully balanced wines, the amiable hosts-all combine to create a special moment in time, above a hidden valley, on the side of a sun-drenched mountain. Moss Vineyards rewards anyone who takes the path less traveled.

Proprietor: Chris Yordy
Winemaker: Fritz Repich
Year Established: 2004

MOUNTFAIR VINEYARDS

Mountfair Vineyards
A Winery with a Special Vibe

By: Bit Pressley

Every season brings something special when you live near the Blue Ridge Mountains. In the spring, I never need much of an excuse to take a weekend drive in the country. Sometimes my route takes me up 810, where, a few miles past the crossroads of White Hall and a bit off of the beaten path, it just so happens Mountfair Vineyards is located. A proud member of the Monticello Wine Trail, Mountfair is a hidden treasure with excellent wine and all the excuse you need to take a drive in the country. A small winery with about 5 acres of grapes, Mountfair specializes in producing a variety of blends based of the traditional Bordeaux grapes: Merlot, Cabernet Sauvignon, Cabernet Franc, Petit Verdot, and Malbec. Such descriptions, however, do not begin to define the essence of the place.

One recent early spring evening, as friends and family of Mountfair sat around a communal dinner table in the winery's barrel room, enjoying potluck dishes amidst the ambiance of candlelight and aging wine, the conversation landed on that very topic. Inevitably, the "who are we?" question was posed. Adjectives flew but no concurring opinion settled the matter entirely. One thing is for sure: everyone agreed Mountfair is not your typical winery.

Warm, unpretentious, eclectic and familial are all fitting words used to describe the "Mountfair vibe," that feeling you get with this winery that comes when you first see it and get to know the people who run it and, most especially, when you partake of the fruits of their labor. A feeling which seems to envelope you like spring sun on your face after a particularly long and dreary winter. From the moment you walk into the tasting room, you are greeted as an old friend and regaled with stories behind the quirky wine names – Wooloomooloo (named after a mythical spirit said to roam the Blue Ridge Mountains), Jilted (you'll have to hear that story from the source), and Blended Family (describing the blending of grapes or, better still, the blending of two families as a result of a certain upcoming nuptial). Each wine reflects the unique nature and complexity their respective name implies. Each receive a healthy dose of oak aging resulting in an interestingly complex, age-worthy wine sure to only improve with time. And each is a real treat for lovers of Bordeaux grape varietals and blends. Mountfair Vineyards is a small artisanal winery specializing in red Bordeaux-style blends only, but they try to offer something for all tastes. Several friends of the winery - local wine and cider makers who don't have tasting rooms - are featured as well. As such, a tasting could include ciders, sparklers and white wines, in addition to fabulous reds!

Located on the eastern slope of the Blue Ridge Mountains northwest of Charlottesville, Mountfair emphasizes small lot viticulture and small batch fermentation methods in the making of wine. An organic endeavor from the beginning, Mountfair started years ago as a horse farm. Chris Yordy bought 30 acres on Fox Mountain in 1991, building a farmhouse on the top of the property and a horse barn next to the road. In 1998, while working for Cisco Systems, he met Fritz Repich. The two IT guys became fast friends, sharing many a bottle of wine and, eventually, an interest in winemaking. As luck would have it, Chris' land happened to be in the middle of a burgeoning Virginia wine industry. Moreover, further inspection confirmed that soil conditions were just right: grapes - good wine grapes – would grow on the land. So Chris and Fritz started experimenting with planting grape vines; their first was in 2004. Chris will tell you that none of the initial vines survived, but half of the next year's plantings took, making it "a success story." From there he never looked back as his horse farm transformed into a vineyard.

The horse barn was a perfect spot for a tasting room. Its conversion began in 2007 and was completed a year later. Chris, trained in the timber framing method of construction, harvested trees from the property to create the distinctive frame; carefully fitted and joined timbers with joints secured by large wooden pegs. Oak slats from the horse stalls were cleaned and reused as the ceiling of the tasting room. The tasting room bar is made from used oak barrels topped with a wood counter made from the same indigenous white pine used in the rest of the building.

Walk past the tasting room into the barrel room and you'll see oak barrels stacked, containing two years worth of single varietals. Each wine at Mountfair (remember, they only make reds) is aged in oak barrels for up to two years. The barrel room does double duty as an event space, with a small stage for singer/songwriter acoustic performers. Tables topped with flickering candles make the space welcoming and intimate. Since the barrel room also serves as the primary winemaking room (and bottling room four times a year), you might see Fritz, who now carries the title of winemaker as well as part owner, creating fantastic Bordeaux blends, checking on the wine or using the barrel thief to do a sampling for some lucky customer.

A patio with spectacular views of the Blue Ridge Mountains is located just off the tasting room and the perfect place to enjoy a glass of wine. Since you are in the country, it is no surprise that wildlife abounds; you may spot the local blue heron (or the visiting osprey or king fisher) looking for dinner at the nearby pond, or catch the song of the red-winged black bird as he calls his mate, or watch a wine club member snag a large mouthed bass (fishing privileges are among the perks of membership). Bring a picnic and enjoy the beauty and serenity of the land that supports the winery and become a part of the Mountfair vibe.

The people, the architecture, artisanship of the tasting room and the beauty of the surrounding countryside all combine to create an inviting and memorable ambiance, but in the end, it is the wine that leaves an indelible impression on visitors. Mountfair focuses on high quality, low quantity boutique Bordeaux-style red blends using a variety of classic grapes and they do it right. Some of Virginia's finest red wines are made at this little winery. As one customer remarked, "this could be Napa, thirty years ago." Their blends reflect a distinctive winemaking style; smooth, balanced, low tannins, with a lingering finish that experienced patrons know will quickly sell out. So do yourself a favor and take a ride in the country to find your way to a little winery with a very special vibe.

Owners: Dean and Lynn Easton Andrews
Winemaker: Michael Shaps
Year Established: 2010

PIPPIN HILL FARM
& *vineyards*

Pippin Hill Farm & Vineyards
Elegance and Simplicity

By: Justin Stone

Imagine sitting under a veranda overlooking pristine foothills back-dropped by the Blue Ridge Mountains. There's a glass of Virginia wine and fire-baked artisanal pizza on the table before you, banks of native flora edging the landscaped grounds and local musicians lending their sounds to the tone of the afternoon. This is just one of the idyllic experiences waiting for you at Pippin Hill Farm and Winery. It may be the youngest winery in the Monticello region, but its owners, Dean and Lynn Easton Andrews, are applying lessons learned through their years at the top of the hospitality industry. At Pippin Hill, they have merged their talents to create a boutique winery that provides its visitors with a true Virginia experience.

Every aspect of Pippin Hill is meant to enhance the experience of its visitors while taking advantage of the natural surroundings. Dean and Lynn ensure that the philosophy and practices of their farm-winery adhere to the principles of sustainability. The farm's gardens provide the kitchen and winery with an array of seasonal herbs, vegetables, and flowers and all production waste is turned back into the farm's ecosystem. The full-scale vineyard-to-table kitchen provides guests with exquisite local cuisine for a quick afternoon snack or a fine, multi-course dinner. Eighty percent of the food is sourced locally from Pippin Hill Farm or other area farms.

Native grasses, plants, trees and the carefully thought-out buildings blend together in the natural landscape to create a picturesque location for events. The interior settings provide a range of possibilities for guests, from intimate gatherings in the Cellar to extravagant celebrations in the Granary. Despite having only recently opened its doors in the spring of 2011, Pippin Hill is already a premier destination and event space, not surprising when considering the collaborative talents of its owners.

Dean spent over thirty years at the top of the hospitality industry. While vice-president of the prestigious Orient-Express Hotels, he oversaw operations of internationally renowned resorts and restaurants. He directed the acquisition and renovation of the famed 21 Club in New York along with the purchase of Keswick Hall and Club in 1999. It was the Keswick venture that ultimately led him to settle in the Charlottesville area. Lynn began her professional career in the television industry as an associate producer and producer for NBC, ABC, and CNN News. She relocated to Charlottesville in 1989 and transitioned naturally to the production of events. As founder and president of Charlottesville-based Easton Events, she has built a premier event planning company that now spans the mid-Atlantic region.

Chris Hill and Michael Shaps were two of the Virginia wine experts called upon by the Andrews to begin the vineyard. With guidance from these experts' decades of experience in the industry, the Andrews chose to plant three signature varietals at Pippin Hill. These young vines of Sauvignon Blanc, Chardonnay, and Petit Verdot line the southern hillsides below the winery. The Andrews intentionally keep their vineyard small while partnering with local growers to supply them with grapes from the greater Piedmont region. This will give them greater versatility and security in a region known for its inconsistent seasons.

Chris Hill, a consultant for dozens of vineyards in the Albemarle region, oversees the management of the six acres of vines at Pippin Hill. The Andrews rely on the skill and resources of Michael Shaps and his Virginia Wineworks facility to produce, bottle, and label their wines. Dean, Michael, and Chris consult routinely on the status of the grapes and development of the wines. The result of this collaboration is a first vintage of Pippin Hill wines that are approachable and enjoyable while reflecting the local flavor.

It is the Andrews' intention for Pippin Hill to maintain a perfect balance between sought-after event site and well-respected producer of Virginia wines. With the fresh exuberance that stems from the seasoned staff and their own zeal for this new venture, Dean and Lynn are confident that Pippin Hill will take its place among Virginia's storied wineries. As an indication of their promising future, they were asked to join the Monticello Wine Trail in their first year, and their event spaces have been routinely booked since opening.

The Andrews have also initiated a new tourism trail for the Southern region. The Jefferson Heritage Trail will span between Thomas Jefferson's Monticello home and his Poplar Forest home in Lynchburg. Along the trail, wineries, microbreweries, restaurants, and inns of the region will welcome visitors and delight them with the bounty and beauty of Virginia. Youth is not often seen as a virtue in the wine industry but, in the case of the Andrews and their Pippin Hill Farm and Winery, the excitement of a new venture has been paired with the wisdom of age and experience.

Owners: David and Margo Pollak
Winemaker: Ben Pineu
Year Established: 2008

POLLAK
VINEYARDS

Pollak Vineyards
Building on Traditions in Rockfish Gap

By: Justin Stone

The unmarked dapple-gray pavement of Route 796 forks off from the well-worn blacktop of Rt. 250 West just before the latter rises up and passes over the Blue Ridge Parkway. This weathered country road demands an abrupt downshift in pace. Instead of cruising over the pastoral landscape, travelers find themselves meandering through it. Lush overgrowth obscures a brook to the left; a few wooded driveways emerge discreetly on the right to meet the road. A sign with the familiar text and image denoting a Virginia winery directs traffic onto an equally rustic roadway that appears to end at the base of the mountain backdrop rising ahead. Suddenly, the wooded lots and country homes give way to an open stretch of gently rising hillsides. There, in the shadow of the Rockfish Gap Valley, is Pollak Vineyards.

Its owners, David and Margo Pollak, understood the power of the view when they searched for their perfect farm. They had experienced that same draw while driving through the wine regions of the West Coast and Europe. To Margo's chagrin, David would often pause during their travels, pull over, and gaze at the trellised acres of vinifera vines with a yearning eye.

The roots of David's desire to found his own vineyard were planted over twenty years prior. During the mid-70s he had helped expand vineyards in California's developing Russian River Valley. Then, in 1981, while working as an executive for DuPont, David formed a small partnership that acquired and rejuvenated a pre-Prohibition era winery in the neglected Carneros District of California. Considered a great risk at the time, today the Bouchaine Winery is credited with developing the Burgundian style of wines for which Carneros is renowned. During the early '90s, David sold off his interests in California wines and traveled with Margo through the great wine countries of Europe. Those travels intensified David's desire for a vineyard of his own. When he and Margo returned, they began an intensive six-year pursuit for the ideal location to plant their vines.

After many unsuccessful drives through Ohio, Washington, and California, friends pointed them to Virginia, which was being called the Napa of the East Coast. David and Margo enlisted the aid of veteran consultants Christopher Hill and Michael Shaps to help find something suitable in the Virginia region. The two industry stalwarts directed them to a former organic vegetable farm on the southern base of Afton Mountain. When David and Margo came across the property in 2001 they knew immediately it was worth stopping for.

A picturesque lake and dramatic views of the Blue Ridge greeted them. Testing proved that the property had the unique charactcristics ideal for the natural cultivation of grapes. According to geographic vernacular, Pollak sits at the base of a "wind gap," a dried streambed that previously cut across a mountain range. It is regionally known as Rockfish Gap and provides the vineyard with consistent breezes that prevent rot and disease. The property also contains several microclimates, each with distinct soil composition and variant ambient conditions. These "blocks," as referenced by the Pollak staff, allow for detailed varietal selection and placement in the vineyard. The attentive focus on the details of the land and vines defines David's philosophy for his vineyard and seems instilled in every member of the Pollak Vineyards family.

From General Manager Nick Dovel to Vineyard Manager Chris Zwadlo, there is a committed effort to making the best wines possible. When their celebrated Meritage is being blended in the winery, Nick, Chris, the winemakers, and Dave are present. Each worker tastes the wine from its barrel and weighs in on the final makeup of the complex blend.

From the beginning, everyone involved with Pollak has been committed to the best agricultural and winemaking practices. They practice dry farming, a non-irrigated methodology that relies exclusively on rain and seeks to cultivate vigorous vines through natural stressing. It is a risky practice in a region known for its seasonal droughts but the benefit is hearty vines with maturity and depth to their fruit and complexity in the wines.

© *Elizabeth Flood*

The trellis system at Pollak is referred to as a Smart (after the Australian doctor who created it) or Ballerina (due to the pirouette shape of the trained vines) trellis. It keeps the vines open, allowing air to dry the grapes. It is a system that exemplifies the understanding of the land and dedication to viticulture characteristic of Pollak.

Just as their setting demands attention, their wines have been widely recognized as some of the finest in the region. In 2010, the Monticello Wine Competition awarded

Pollak's Petite Verdot with their highest distinction, the Monticello Cup. This past year they were awarded "Best Small Winery" at the Riverside International Wine Competition in Riverside, California. 2011 also saw three of their wines earn scores of 93 points by the Beverage Testing Institute in Chicago. This level of acclaim has often been reserved for vineyards several decades into their establishment.

Recently, David modestly acknowledged to the Virginia Wine Gazette that Pollak is no pioneer; "The winemaker pioneers in Virginia figured out what works here and what doesn't work here in terms of grape varieties. Now we have a chance to take the knowledge of the pioneers from the '70s and combine that with some modern winemaking and vineyard techniques and really move ahead in this business."

Move ahead they will. As a young winery, Pollak has excelled at building upon the experience of older Virginia wineries, refining particular practices and varietals in Virginia to produce world-class wines. David's early California Carneros success seems to be repeating itself in the Monticello region. Expect Pollak to continue to inspire awe from the roadside and the tableside.

Owner: Kristin Swanson Holzman
Winemaker: Brad Hansen
Year Established: 1982 (purchased by Holzman in 2005)

Prince Michel Vineyard & Winery

Fulfilling a New Vision While Embracing a Proud History

By: Boo Barnett

Prince Michel Vineyard & Winery was founded in 1982 by Jean and Silvian LeDucq, respected pioneers in the burgeoning Virginia wine industry at the time, and credited with incorporating Old World techniques for making wine with New World fruit, creating a successful "Old World" winery on the East Coast. Today, Prince Michel is one of the largest wineries in the state as well as on the east coast, producing and widely distributing some forty thousand cases of wine a year. Located north of Charlottesville, the winery is home to both the Prince Michel and Rapidan River labels.

Kristin Swanson Holzman acquired Prince Michel in 2005. With a flair for marketing and an entrepreneurial spirit, she is a major factor in the success and growth of Prince Michel. Kristin had no background in the industry before purchasing the winery. A professional designer of luxury yacht interiors, her first step into the wine business came when she purchased an historic Ivy estate planted with robust Viognier vines. Selling grapes from those established vineyards introduced Kristin to Chris Hill and Brad Hansen. The relationship with these wine professionals led her to purchase Prince Michel, making her one of the few female vineyard owners. Her extensive marketing experience and business savviness shows in every aspect of the operation.

Three twirling metal wine glass wind sculptures out front greet visitors and are the signature landmark. The building itself is right off of Route 29, serving to attract large numbers of tourists and locals visiting wineries in the area as well as shoppers or commuters heading to or from Washington, D.C. As you enter, walk past a small wine museum and through a gift gallery to get to the tasting room, which doubles as a gift shop. In the center, amid an array of gifts and novelty souvenirs, is a circular bar where attentive servers recite succinct wine descriptions as they pour, covering the basics of the tastings offered. $5 will cover a tasting of nearly 15 wines. There are also wine slushies for those who feel adventurous, as well as the occasional baked good featuring various vintages.

Although not a minimalist presentation, the staff does not generally linger to entertain with their knowledge of wine, or of varietals, or particular methodologies and techniques, especially when the place is hopping, as is often the case. In addition to shopping and wine tasting, visitors can take a free self-guided tour that starts from the rear of the tasting room. The staff will arrange guided tours through the cellars and vineyard for a fee, and supply snacks for an additional cost. Advanced reservations are encouraged for guided tours (and please note that these tours are not handicap accessible). The winery is family friendly, but moms and dads should be mindful of the many shelves of knickknacks for sale that make for an irresistible temptation for little fingers.

Prince Michel has a long list of awards. Bottles hung with medal ribbons are proudly displayed throughout the facility. Their Cabernet Franc and Barrel Select Chardonnay are the most decorated. With the amount of wine produced, Prince Michel tends to offer something for everyone. Their philosophy is to make the best wine they can and in so doing attract repeat customers; a business model that balances value, quality and consistency. This is a large volume operation and they make no apologies for it, shipping wine to every state where they can legally do so. They also design custom labels for individuals, which is always a fun gift idea for that special someone.

Of course, to produce such quantity takes a lot of grapes. Though sturdy rows of vines surround the building, most of the wines are made from non-estate grown grapes. Examples include Chardonnay and Merlot from Mt. Juliet, while Quaker Run, Crown Winery, and others vineyards provide Petit Verdot, Cabernet Franc, Petit Manseng, Cabernet Sauvignon, Pinot Grigio, Syrah and others. In fact, in order to keep up with demand for the Rapidan River wines, they purchase some of their grapes from out of state.

In addition to wine production and extensive gift sales, Prince Michel promotes its wedding business. While there is no grand hall nor expansive baronial ballroom, couples can choose from the intimate courtyard, the barrel caves, or the sloping lawn next to the vineyard for their wedding. Luxury suites are available for weddings or romantic weekend getaways. Such spaces are also offered for corporate events, family reunions, and other celebrations.

Prince Michel is now partnering with Charlottesville's Carter's Mountain Orchard and has established a tasting room in the shadow of Mr. Jefferson's mountain home. This new tasting room is bound to attract folks who want to try the latest vintage while taking in the unmatchable views of Carter's Mountain.

Prince Michel has a proud heritage and is an important part of the history of Virginia wine. Prince Michel embraces this proud history, but is not hindered by it. As such, the Old World winery of the East Coast is a major exporter of Virginia wine, bringing consistent quality wine at affordable prices to well established oenophiles and wine novices alike throughout Virginia and the world.

©Elizabeth Flood

119

Owners: Roe and Dee Allison
Winemaker/Consultant: Michael Shaps
Vineyard Consultant: Chris Hill
Year Established: 2006

Reynard Florence
Virginia Family Farm Creating New Traditions
By: Boo Barnett

Reynard Florence is one of the newest Orange County vineyards. Although the business is new to the area, Roe and Dee Allison are natives, with family history tying them to the region. For this second career, they built on their degrees from the University of Virginia and Mary Baldwin with certification in Enology and Viticulture, and immediately put their knowledge to work on their farm.

Planted on an eastern slope to minimize frost and afternoon sun scorch damage, grapes are trained on a special Ballerina trellis. Mr. Allison, whose carpentry skills came to the fore here, established proper spacing and 9' high supports for maximum sun exposure, ventilated growth and ease of canopy management. This is particularly important for their Grenache, a tightly clustered grape that might otherwise fail during the Commonwealth's sultry summers. Their rocky soil provides just the right drainage and mineral content for these carefully selected varietals.

Petit Manseng, their recent Virginia State Fair gold, was planted in 2006. From a similar horticultural environment in southwest France, this grape flourishes at Reynard Florence. Currently, in addition to the Petit Manseng, they offer the following: Cabernet Franc, Grenache, Merlot, Malbec and a Blanc comprised of Riesling, Traminette, Petit Verdot and Viognier. As a boutique winery, they have chosen to concentrate on quality over quantity, producing 500 cases, with the possibility of ramping up to 1000. They also hired the finest experts at the start: the guiding hands of Chris Hill and Michael Shaps are evident throughout the vineyard.

The bright, clean tasting room features a large Picasso wall hanging holding court over a warm wood and yellow toned interior. Outside of the tasting room is a sunny patio with tables perfect for enjoying a picnic, their wonderful wines, and the spectacular view. Visitors may also relax on the shaded porch and patio at the side of the tasting room.

Adding an old fashioned touch, Rosés bloom at the end of each vine row. Beside adding beauty and drawing in pollinators, the Rosés serve a practical horticultural purpose as an early warning system for some diseases. Should the Rosés sicken, the farmer knows to address the problem quickly before it takes over the entire field.

Close to some other notable and much larger vineyards, Reynard Florence holds its own with its small but thoughtfully considered offerings. This is a labor of love for the Allisons, whose enthusiasm and Southern hospitality help make a visit to Reynard Florence a memorable one.

Owner: Scott Stinson
Winemakers: Scott and Rachel Stinson
Year Established: 2009

Stinson Vineyards
A Family Affair

By: Gayle Davies

Drawn to the property primarily because of interest in the residence, the Stinsons came into being vintners accidentally. Scott Stinson, an architect from Northern Virginia/D.C., focused much of his work on historic architecture and restoration. With a personal preference for historic homes and his wife Martha's desire to relocate in Albemarle County, they spent four years scouring the area for the perfect restoration-worthy house. In 2009, they found and purchased the Piedmont House located at the base of Sugar Hollow in the tiny town of White Hall, which is nestled in the foothills of the Blue Ridge Mountains.

Built in 1796, with an addition in 1850, the house looks much as it did to General Thomas "Stonewall" Jackson and his six thousand troops when, according to local lore, they slept in a nearby field during the Valley Campaign of 1862. Fate intervened shortly after Scott and Martha moved into the historic old house when they noticed a vineyard in those same fields where General Jackson's army probably camped. They began to ponder the possibilities. Originally, there were no plans to start a winery before purchasing the property, but looking out over those vineyards they began to think, "Well, why not?"

Scott and Martha's romantic notions of having an interesting family business took shape. The family's combination of talents and interests proved well-suited for creating such a family business in the form of a boutique winery.

Scott and Martha enlisted the help of their two talented daughters, Rachel and Rebecca. Rachel had been living in New York for five years as a professional photographer. When approached with the idea, Rachel thought long and hard about leaving her close-knit community and cosmopolitan life. In the end, she decided that it was best to work towards growing a family business rather than building one for someone else, so she moved here in December of 2009 to begin her role as winemaker. As an artist, the project held real appeal. Other food-related passions, particularly the burgeoning locavore movement, offered additional incentive. Now as a result of her vision, you can purchase quality local meats from Stinson in addition to wine.

The second daughter, Rebecca, also had a strong interest in growing food and cooking, so naturally she followed her sister into the family business a year later. Rebecca manages the tasting room at the winery, and the family benefits greatly from her efforts. The hard work and enthusiasm that she brings to the family business is apparent throughout the year as Rebecca plans and hosts the many fun events at Stinson Vineyards.

Martha Stinson is an avid gardener. You could say she is a born expert. Her flowers beautify the grounds around the historic house as well as the tasting room and her expertise with growing tomatoes and other vegetables made for a nice transition to tending vines. It is not surprising to see how she contributes to the family business. She is devoted to the vineyards and finds her duties expanding as her experience, the vines, and their acreage grow. Lucky visitors might even get the opportunity to meet the gentle, soft-spoken matriarch and purchase her beautiful produce when in season.

Naturally, Scott's career in architecture was a real benefit in creating an appealing look for their facilities. Playing on the *vins du garages* movement out of Bordeaux, France, Scott redesigned the existing garage to create a contemporary, stylish tasting room and winery building. It is quite an intimate and welcoming space. Similarly, Rachel's artistic training gave vision to the distinct graphics used on their labels, signs and other materials.

While the look is modern, the winemaking techniques used at Stinson are very traditional and the results impressive. Rather than going the custom crush route like many start-up wineries, the Stinsons bought state-of-the-art-equipment right at the beginning. This father-daughter wine team knew that to become experts in any field requires consultation and interaction with other experts. To that end, they asked Mathieu Finot, the well-known head winemaker for King Family Vineyards, to assist Rachel in her process of learning to make quality Virginia wines. Matthieu's traditional French background influenced the style of wines made at Stinson, as seen in the winery and vineyard operations generally, right down to the decision to use all-

French tanks and barrels. Virginia wine making is a family enterprise in more ways than one. It is common to see local winery owners and wine makers helping each other in their work because all efforts build the quality and reputation of this region.

In addition to Mattheiu's mentoring, Rachel immersed herself in viticulture and enology by taking courses with Greg Rosko at Piedmont Community College. This coursework proved useful when the Stinsons had to replant ailing vines. They are not discouraged, however, because they know setbacks are to be expected in an industry comprised of a unique combination of science, art and frankly, luck. So, while waiting for the newly planted vines to mature, their fruit is currently purchased from other local vineyards (also not uncommon in the industry). They are currently making Sauvignon Blanc, Rosé, Chardonnay, Sugar Hollow White, Petit Manseng, Cabernet Franc and Meritage.

Stinson is located in Sugar Hollow, one of the most beautiful places on Earth. This wonderful and historic spot, with sweeping views of the mountains in the Shenandoah Park (and Buck's Elbow to the south), provides the perfect setting to enjoy the wines at Stinson Vineyards, ideally with great friends and a picnic basket. Stop by and become a part of their family business.

129

Owners: The Breiner family
Winemaker: Peter Rausse
Year established: 1995

STONE MOUNTAIN VINEYARDS

Stone Mountain Vineyards
Delicious Wine for the Daring

By: Boo Barnett

Al Breiner used to wonder out loud if he should charge for the viewings and give away the wine. At an elevation of 1700 feet up in the Blue Ridge Mountains, Stone Mountain Vineyards provides a memorable, windswept panorama. Inspired by the Rhine River Valley's steep vineyards, the Breiner family decided to bring high altitude, slope-clinging grapes to rural Dyke, Virginia. Al and his son Chris brought this vision into reality, planting the first seeds in 1995.

Every part of the design here turns the steep slope challenge into an advantage. Out on the mountain, wind streams keep the mildew at a minimum, while blowing away early and late season frosts. The tasting room is set back into the hill so as not to disturb the view, as well as to create a naturally cooled cave below, 55 degrees with constant humidity. The sideways terrain demands handpicking, and that select harvesting means only the best bunches are picked, leading to a high quality, low quantity product. Even the winery uses the vertiginous site well: Chris Breiner designed a maximum gravity flow processing within the wine cave.

Like some of the lowland Virginia vintners, Al opted for a more Italian approach to winemaking, and hired Gabriele Rausse as the guiding light. After Al passed away in 2002, Chris became the face of Stone Mountain Vineyards and took over as winemaker and managing partner until 2012, while Gabriele stayed on as a consultant. The Breiner/Rausse wines have won a long list of prizes over the years: Governor's Cups, Tasters' Guild International Awards, Vinifera Growers' Awards, etc. They feature Cabernet Franc, Cabernet Sauvignon, Chardonnay, Petit Verdot, Viognier, Malbec and several blends including Bacon Hollow Revenuer's Select and Maquillage.

The tasting room is large and uncluttered, with hardwood floors and a bar made of reclaimed heart pine boards. As well-crafted as it is, it cannot compete with the view from the observation deck. Get your glass and gaze over the valley stretched out far, far below you. Then take a tour into the cave; it really deepens your experience (just make sure to bring a sweater!). Also bring a picnic, though boxed food is available for purchase there on Saturdays and Sundays. You've come all this way and will not want to face the drive back down on an empty stomach.

A word about the road in – they used to sell caps that ask, "How 'bout that road in?" It is STEEP, winding, unpaved, extremely narrow without guardrails and in inclement weather, daunting. When you get to the top, remarked a fellow guest, you *need* a drink. The wilderness aspects of this site are furthered by wildlife sightings including bear, deer and rafters of turkey. To keep the wildlife from eating the grapes, the vineyard also has imposing (but friendly) dogs.

There are two guesthouses available for rent, which are quiet, even alpine in their simplicity. If you want to experience a remote vineyard setting that is really only one harrowing car ride from civilization, this is it. Nothing high tech, either—just you, the winds and the vineyard. Oh yea, and don't forget the great wine.

Sadly, the Virginia wine industry and wine enthusiasts everywhere lost Chris Breiner on February 14, 2012, when he died unexpectedly. Fellow winery owner Dennis Horton said, "Chris was one of the good guys in the Virginia wine industry. You knew where you stood with Chris and he always, always, did exactly what he said he would do. I will miss him tremendously." Chris had shared his father's love of agriculture and rural land, and had continued the vision for the vineyard and winery, which that love had inspired. Chris' all too short life was spent in the efforts to see that shared dream become a reality.

Today the Breiner Family's wine legacy continues under the management of Chris's niece, Kate Breiner. As a third generation wine grower, Kate works as General Manager and Assistant Winemaker, and upholds the tradition and passion set forth by her grandfather and uncle. Gabriele Rausse's son Peter also joined the Stone Mountain team as winemaker during this time of transition.

Stone Mountain Vineyards stands largely as a result of Chris Breiner's vision, hard work, dedication and perseverance. In addition to the legacy of the vineyard, the wine industry recently established the Chris Breiner Memorial Scholarship for PVCC's Viticulture program, as a way to honor Chris by supporting promising young vintners. As Kate Breiner and Peter Rausse continue the work begun by their predecessors, they continue to establish Stone Mountain's unique place within the central Virginia Wine country, and they honor the lives and vision of Chris and Al.

Owner: Eric Trump Wine Manufacturing LLC
Winemakers: Katel Griaud (still wines), Jonathan
Wheeler (sparkling)
Year Established: 1999 as Kluge Winery & Vineyard,
2011 as Trump Winery

Trump Winery
Creating New World wines inspired by a deep Old World tradition.
By: Andy Josselyn

Eric Trump and his family's mantra of producing the highest quality product at the forefront of the marketplace could not be better served than at Trump Winery. The wine has been winning significant accolades including multiple gold medals on a national and international scale, and Eric himself was named a Rising Star in the wine industry by Wine Enthusiast magazine in 2013, to name a few recent accomplishments. This bright future is not without a dramatic past, however. The story of Trump Winery is one of redemption and revival; it is the rebirth of what was one of the most ambitious undertakings in modern Virginia wine history.

One cannot start to tell the tale of what is now Trump Winery without first visiting what has come before. Patricia Kluge and her husband William Moses planted the first vines on the estate in 1999 with the goal of bringing international attention and acclaim for what Virginia wine could be. They invested heavily in all areas of the business, planted the largest vineyard in Virginia (just under 200 acres) and built state of the art production, aging and bottling facilities, all on site. World-class vineyard consultants like Michel Rolland and Laurent Champs were brought in, and the ubiquitous Gabriele Rausse oversaw the planting of vines and winemaking for a time. Unfortunately, the heavy investing, high volume production and winemaking superstar line up did not keep up with market circumstances, and in late 2009 the property went into bank receivership before being purchased by the Trump in 2011. Based on a powerful vision, Patricia Kluge set the stage for what continues to be a future filled with bright promise for Trump Winery.

Eric Trump and General Manager Kerry Woolard have been very selective about what changes were made in the vineyard and the winery, retaining much of what worked well in the Kluge-era. There has been a significant effort to hire local, experienced folks in the tasting room and operations side of the business, and reaching out to connect with other wineries on the Monticello Trail has become a priority. The focus on making the highest quality wines has never wavered, but in addition to making their own wine, Trump is now one of the largest providers of grapes to area wineries, a practice that fully takes advantage of the sprawling estate. The tasting room has been renovated to reflect a more traditional tasting experience, and now offers stunning views of the vineyard from the back patio. Thoughts of glitz and glamour quickly melt away the moment a friendly member of the tasting room staff welcomes you up to the bar, where upon your first sip, one can see some things have thankfully remained the same.

Eric wisely sought to keep winemakers Jonathan Wheeler and Katell Griaud on after completing the changeover. Wheeler is the head of the sparkling wine program, and continues to win awards with his bubbly, including a gold medal at San Francisco International Wine Competition, best-in-class at the Jefferson Cup Invitational for his 2008 Blanc de Blanc and a score of 91 points in

Wine Enthusiast for his 2007 Sparkling Reserve in 2013, the highest a Virginia wine had ever rated in the prestigious magazine. Griaud is the head of the still wine program, and she too is winning medals and awards. Her roots are in Bordeaux (she is a third generation member of a family of Bordeaux wine makers), and nowhere does this heritage show more than in her big red Bordeaux-style blends, delicate dry whites and her delightful Provence-style Rosé.

It has been said that Virginia's terroir, in many ways, has more in common with the Old World of wine, places like Bordeaux and Champagne, than it does with familiar spots in the New World. That truth shines through brightly in the wines of Trump, where the tasting notes are filled with references to Old World techniques like French Oak and "on the lees" aging and the fascinating *méthode champenoise.* (ask a knowledgeable tasting room associate if you don't know what these techniques entail!). Yet as you get a glass, a delicious BLT sandwich and head towards the back patio and look out over the stunning vista, there is no other place you could possibly be than the rolling hills of the Virginia Blue Ridge. It is here, just down the road from Jefferson's Monticello, that one can see where the future of the New World wine tradition touches its beginnings and connects to a past deeply rooted in the mythic origins of the vine. And if the view over the Trump vineyard on a mild summer evening is anything to go by, the future of Monticello area winemaking is very bright indeed.

Owners: Andrew and Patricia Hodson
Winemakers: Emily Pelton, Andrew Hodson
Year Established: 1999

Veritas Vineyard & Winery

Truth Found in a Leap of Faith

By: Justin Stone

Andrew Hodson is the patriarch of Veritas Vineyard & Winery. As a young man he dedicated his life to medicine, working in Pennsylvania, North Carolina, and Florida. A talented neurologist, his hands became an expression of his intellect, compassion, and skill. Medicine was his passion, shared with his wife, Patricia, who owned a medical billing service, but in the 1990s, the couple decided to leave the profession. They were looking for something new, something to bring change to each year and each season. They didn't know then, but their choice brought a great change in which the seasons are celebrated by "each vintage."

A ndrew describes his transition to vintner as a perfect segue. A casual visit to Virginia's wine country led to the purchase of Saddleback farm. Soon after, the family sold their homes in the South and arranged the move North. "There was just no doubt about it," said Andrew about the decision. While practicing medicine in Philadelphia, the Hodsons often went camping in Virginia's Blue Ridge Mountains. Looking back, Andrew believes something in those family memories encouraged the decision that changed their lives.

Daughters Emily and Chloe held down the farm the first year. Andrew and Patricia spent most of that year in Florida closing down their careers in medicine. The girls, who are twelve years apart, fondly recall learning how to run a farm together as the beginning of the close bond they now share. Whether trapped on the front porch by an overbearing horse or almost taking out the house with a tractor's front end, it was a humorously formidable year for them both. Andrew and Patricia joined their daughters in 1999, in time to see the first vines of Cabernet Franc, Merlot, Traminette, Tanat, and Petite Verdot planted, adding Viognier, Sauvignon Blanc, and Manseng the following year. With vines firmly rooted, Veritas Vineyard & Winery, started as the family's labor of love, began to take shape. The name seemed right. Derived from the Roman historian Pliny the Elder's observation: "In Vino Veritas," meaning "In Wine There is Truth," it is a fitting name since Andrew discovered truth can indeed be found in a leap of faith.

In 2002, Veritas opened to the public. Andrew crafted the first vintages with Emily assisting. The process was one of opportunity, taking advantage of lessons learned from the soil, vines, and grapes while relying on judgment to drive the winery's evolution. Emily took over as lead winemaker after the first few years, using her technical understanding of winemaking and Masters of Enology from Virginia Tech that proved instrumental in creating wines that are among the best in Virginia. Her skill and dedication to winemaking were recognized in 2007 when she was awarded the title of Overall Winner in the Women Winemakers Challenge at the National Women's Wine Competition. Her Viognier – made from a grape quickly becoming the signature grape of Virginia - is one of the finest examples coming from the Monticello AVA. Although Andrew's presence in the winery continues to be influential to the wine's development, he and Patricia are semiretired. Undoubtedly, they rest comfortably in the knowledge that the family winery is in good hands.

Veritas was not originally intended to be an event destination. Initially, wine tastings occurred on picnic tables out on the lawn, but Patricia saw how much people enjoyed the setting and went to work designing the tasting room and grounds. Her design is open and versatile, allowing guests to experience Veritas wines in an extraordinary place with elegant décor and artwork, giving the space an Elizabethan feel. Visitors enjoy wine outside, from the porch or picnic tables and Adirondack chairs on the lawn featuring breathtaking views. Guests also relax inside on hearthside couches and chairs across from a warm fire softly glowing. No wonder people from all over flock to this special place for weddings, parties and concerts, or to relax in such a pristine setting. Because of the popularity of their wines and a reputation for being one of the best event destinations in the region, Veritas currently produces 12,000 cases of wine per year and hosts thousands of people each season for weddings and other events.

Since Andrew and Patricia are retiring, stewardship of Veritas will pass to their children. Emily hopes to continue the evolution of the varietals and wines produced. Given her track record, success seems inevitable. Their son, George, joined the family business as general manager, helping

Patricia with the finances and managing the tasting room. Chloe insisted she would leave when she grew up, but did give in to the enticement of the family vines for a time. Graduating from the University of Virginia, she worked in the field for a year before taking over event management for the winery. Determined to make good on her promise to see the world outside of Afton, she eventually moved to New York to train as a yoga instructor. Perhaps she will return to take her place in the family business, but whatever the fates have in store for Chloe, the hard work and dedication she brought during her tenure live on in many of the events and traditions she established, such as the wildly popular Starry Nights outdoor concert series.

Veritas is expanding, with a Bed and Breakfast in the Farmhouse and an additional twenty-five acres of vines planted. The family and staff happily measure their lives by "each vintage" produced and enthusiastically enjoy sharing their life's work. Like the name denotes, there is truth to be found in the wine at Veritas, it's an elusive yet palpable truth, the kind that can only be found in a leap of faith.

Owners/Vinters: Michael Shaps and Philip Stafford
Year Established: 2007

WINEWORKS

Michael Shaps

Virginia Wineworks
A Diamond in the Rough

By: Boo Barnett

Now for a hidden gem- Virginia Wineworks! 12 miles south of Charlottesville, in the old Montdomaine spot, Michael Shaps and Philip Stafford (one of the founders of the magical C & O Restaurant) have created a multi-faceted wine industry. Here, Shaps (a Governor's Gold Cup winner) creates wines for his eponymous label, for their Virginia Wineworks line and for private clients... but more on that in a bit. Small signs make sure you arrive at the destination (as you pass First Colony you are almost there) though the almost industrial warehousing and the scrubby woods may give you pause. But don't let the dirt road or the rough exterior make you pass by this Cinderella- here's a clear case of the inside delivering far more than the outside suggests.

Virginia Wineworks is not your standard designer tasting room, ready for brides to pose in front of picturesque vines or hearth. This is a working winery; indeed, they offer the only custom crush service in the Commonwealth and the majority of their output is private label. Tastings are available daily from 11am to 5pm and visitors may select from the

Shaps line, the Wineworks offerings or a combination of the two.

Standard operating procedure at most vineyards includes attractive servers reciting succinct wine descriptions as they pour. These brief wine bios cover the basics of the tastings being offered, sometimes putting them in context of the owner's tastes or the terrior. However, the staff at Wineworks knows wine; not just *their* wine, but wine and you can overhear lively discussions based on thorough knowledge and experience. Lilting French accents, heady smells of fruit and the clicking of soon-to-be-filled bottles create an alluring background score.

Shaps brings his considerable experience to bear here – he is a partner in Maison Shaps et Roucher-Sarrazin, he trained at the Lycee Viticole de Beaune and is still an active winemaker in Burgundy. "In Burgundy," he explains, "the objective is to be true to the appellation and bring out the unique nuances of each site. Here, it is to create a wine that offers mature fruit, concentration, good tannic extraction and enough oak to help the wine develop and age."

A winner of numerous prestigious awards, he travels between France and rural Virginia, employing and educating talented apprentices for the next generation of superb vintners. The difference between his two lines here is well summed up by the owners: Virginia Wineworks is "value oriented with fine, 100% Virginia grapes" while the Shaps line is "produced with traditional Old-World style. (Whites) focus on varietal intensity and retention of natural acidity while (reds) are highly extracted and crafted to be age worthy and require cellaring."

With new wineries popping up all over the Commonwealth, a growing number of businesses open without yet having their own, mature vineyards in production. The solution: Virginia Wineworks custom crush service- they source, craft, bottle, ship and provide licenses, registration and personalized labels for commercial wineries. Everything from the specific grape varietals and type of aging barrel is carefully plotted out- Shaps is the go-to consultant for dozens of producers. This same service is available for individuals. Talk about the ultimate gift for someone who has it all- Virginia Wineworks will create customized wines, based on the client's specific preferences. In-depth conferences provide a profile of customer's taste to design a winemaking plan. The client, who may be completely involved through the entire process, or simply a happy recipient, will have a cellar of unique and finely crafted house wine.

The experience here is that of winemaking: nowhere else do you see the process and appreciate the stages of craft so essential to fine winemaking. There are no grand vistas to distract from the concentrated work that is in full swing before you, and nothing is behind the curtain. At most vineyards, you enjoy a delightful concert. Here, you are at the rehearsals, with your good glass of wine reminding you why so many people take this kind of trouble. If you want to learn about the art and craft of fine wine, or if you simply want to taste an internationally applauded wine in a rustic, no-frills atmosphere, this is it.

I almost hesitate to mention, for obvious reasons, that their most popular wine is in a box. In the ideal world, you would give it a taste without knowing this, decide that it is wonderful for parties, for your daily glass while cooking or as your go-to, "friends drop by" offering – the price is right and the wine is reliable in all the best ways. Then and only then you would see that it is boxed. You either hesitate, wondering if the joke is on you, or you grab about a dozen boxes and swear your friends to secrecy. They are actually too busy grabbing their own dozen boxes to care.

There is a picnic area off under the pines, but it is not for the tick-phobic. You are welcome to use the painted picnic table right outside the warehouse, and (with luck) some of the charming staff may join you.

Owners: Amy Steers, Kathy Rash
Winemaker: Michael Shaps
Year Established: 2000

Well Hung Vineyard

Making Wine That Stands up to Any Occasion

By: Justin Stone

The story of Well Hung Vineyard begins, as any good story must, with the phrase "once upon a time." Yes, that's right, once upon a time there were three women, each with different and unique talents. One day they decided to start a business. But the story of how these three women came together to make their mark on the Virginia wine industry actually starts with a backyard vineyard and an unexpected and unforgettable risqué comment.

Amy Steers awakens each morning to the view of seventeen rows of meticulously kept grapevines stretched across the sloping hilltop of her backyard. The acre-and-a-half of vines were planted in 2000 by Amy and her husband William "Bill" Steers. Bill is a urologist at the University of Virginia Hospital and a long-time wine connoisseur who longed to own a private vineyard. This desire led the family to settle on an idyllic hilltop crest in the Ivy area in the late 1990s.

Amy, a retired nurse, now maintains the neatly cultivated rows of vines. Prior to planting their vines they consulted Gabriele Rausse, who took specs of the property and recommended the exact vineyard site and preferred

151

planting techniques. They decided to grow Chardonnay, Cabernet Franc, Petit Verdot, and Cabernet Sauvignon because of research into Virginia's best performing grapes and their own tastes for the varietals.

By 2001 Amy had a budding vineyard and by 2004 more grapes than she knew what to do with, so she sold grapes to Cardinal Point Winery, who blended them to produce their signature red and white wines. Amy reserved a small batch each year for Bill's experiments in private winemaking, made in an outbuilding that doubles as her gardening shed. One year, a row of Cabernet Franc accidently went unpicked by the harvest crew. It proved a fruitful mistake, for that year Bill made a gorgeous late harvest Cabernet Franc enjoyed by family and friends.

This private winemaking routine went on until 2006, when Amy's friend, Tracy Verkerke, an artist, happened to stop by to visit. Strolling through the vineyard that afternoon, Tracy made an off-handed comment to Amy about the plentiful grapes and how well they hung from the vines. The humorous innuendo was immediately apparent to both and kept them chuckling until they could no longer resist the possibilities the pun suggested. Amy realized that such a colorful name would make for a wonderful wine label, especially given her husband's profession. Amy suggested that they start bottling the grapes they had been growing, and a business was born! By 2008, the harvest of Chardonnay, Cabernet Franc, Cabernet Sauvignon, and Petit Verdot went exclusively into the production of the first bottles of wine for the Well Hung Vineyard label. Photographer Carter Howards, a dear friend of Amy, designed the witty label artwork that holds true to the Winery's name.

Kathy Rash joined the team soon thereafter. Kathy is a local business developer with a head for business and the bottom line. She now lends her financial expertise to Well Hung Vineyard. Her perspective compliments the respective styles and talents of Amy and Tracy. Amy recalls a day in the vineyard that illustrates just how the different views the women bring and lessons they've experienced create the perfect partnership between a nurturing farmer, a spirited artist, and a savvy businesswoman. One summer Kathy observed Amy pruning and thinning the fruit in the vineyard. Seeing the clumps of grape clusters lying in the dirt she exclaimed, "What are you doing? That's money!" Amy chuckled before giving Kathy a genial lesson in basic viticulture, explaining that you have to sacrifice some grapes on the vine in order to intensify the flavor of those remaining. Less is indeed more.

While Amy and Kathy remain the force behind Well Hung as far as tending to the vineyard and marketing the finished product, Tracy has since left the business to pursue her artwork, so they now entrust the winemaking to an industry veteran, Michael Shaps. Each harvest from Amy's backyard vineyard, some three and a half tons of grapes, is hauled to the Virginia Wineworks' custom crush facility. For Amy, the decision to entrust Well Hung wines to Shaps was based on the accessibility of his winery and her faith in his winemaking technique. Michael Shaps has been growing grapes and producing wine in Virginia for over twenty years. His distinct winemaking is a blend of traditional styles producing wines with a softer character than California counterparts but that still possess noticeable oak age and roundness. The decision paid off: their 2010 Chardonnay is delightful, their 2010 Viognier won gold at the recent International Women's Wine Competition, and their 2010 Cabernet Franc won bronze at the 2012 Governor's Cup.

The women behind Well Hung Vineyard seem to have it all: a successful business and an endearing friendship. Where does a small farm vineyard grow from there? They intend to maintain the measured growth that Well Hung has experienced since it began through their participation in wine festivals, which in effect are their "mobile tasting rooms," and their continuing sales with wine retailers in the Charlottesville area and online. The possibility of having their own tasting room has been discussed for the future, but until then, they are content with the status quo, quipping that Well Hung wine stands up to any occasion (pun definitely intended). Amy still reserves enough grapes from each harvest for Bill's private batch, and they still invite friends and family to their annual Harvest Party to help pick grapes and to celebrate the season. Combining a particular blend of realism, optimism, and levity, Well Hung will have much to celebrate in the coming seasons.

Owners: Tony and Edie Champ
Winemaker: Mike Panczak
Year Established: 1992

White Hall Vineyards

New Pioneers in the Blue Ridge Reinvigorate VA Wine

By: Bit Pressley

In Mr. Jefferson's day western Albemarle County was considered part of the western frontier, where pioneers looking to make their home in the Blue Ridge came and settled. The rugged mountains gave the promise of a new life and the excitement of finding opportunity in a bountiful if often dangerous place. Tony and Edie Champ undoubtedly felt such excitement when they moved to Virginia in 1992. Tony and his wife, Edie, developed a love of wine while touring the Napa Valley. They soon became enamored with the idea of starting their own winery and set about looking for the perfect spot to plant vines and build a dream, much as the colonial pioneers who came before them had done. They found paradise: the perfect piece of land located in the crossroads community of White Hall. The area is known for the Moormans River, which flows through Sugar Hollow, and is home to the legendary swimming hole locals affectionately call the "Blue Hole" as well as to the North and South Fork hiking trails. In this idyllic setting, in the shadow of Buck's

Elbow Mountain Range (at the base of the Shenandoah Park), Tony and Edie established White Hall Vineyards.

They came at the perfect time. Virginia wine was really in its infancy. Although Thomas Jefferson attempted to create wine in Virginia throughout his life, he never enjoyed much success. In fact, some of the oldest grape vineyards in Virginia, started as a commercial enterprise, only date back to the mid 1970s, when a few brave souls renewed Jefferson's quest to make great wine in Virginia. These new pioneers who came in the '70s, '80s and early '90s, experimented with varietals through trial and error, and learned how they interacted with the climate and soil conditions in an unforgiving region. Tony and Edie are among those early new pioneers who blazed the trail for others to follow such that there are over 220 wineries and vineyards in Virginia today. When the history of Virginia wine is written, Tony and Edie Champ will be recognized for their early contribution to creating such a successful wine industry in the East.

White Hall vineyard is located at approximately 800 feet of elevation on the eastern slope of the Blue Ridge Mountains and is ideal for viticulture. The grounds around the winery are lovely, with grand old oak trees that shade several picnic tables and offer the visitor a pleasant place to linger over a glass of wine or a bit of lunch. The first six-acres of vines were planted in 1992 and White Hall produced the first vintage as far back as 1994. The vineyard eventually grew to 45-acres but still operates in that same adventurous pioneer spirit that characterized its founding. The Winemaker, Mike Panczak, the driving force behind the quality wines produced at White Hall, often boasts that he likes to try something new every year, whether experimenting with the fermentation process, new yeast or trying a new varietal. He is constantly changing the face of the vineyard, planting new varietals that may stand alone, or compliment others in a blend, occasionally removing varietals that don't thrive or meet his high standards of excellence. His knowledge comes from experience. To make better wine requires experimentation to discover which grapes grow best in a particular vineyard. The only way to truly know is to plant them and see. Although Viognier, the signature grape of Virginia, is his favorite wine to make, White Hall makes over a dozen wines including Chardonnay, Petit Verdot and Cabernet Franc. White Hall also features unique varietals such as Petit Manseng, Touriga Nacional and Gewurztraminer. Visitors may even see Muscat as part of a blend.

White Hall is all about the wine. Although they have an event space on the second floor that is ideal for wine dinners or small weddings, they do not want to be regarded as an event destination so do not foresee a lot of growth in weddings in the years to come. Rather, the family, staff and winemaker at White Hall devote themselves to producing quality wine which has balance and complexity, striving to increase the availability of their wines in Virginia wine shops at affordable price points. As such, their wines are enjoyed throughout the state, nation, and internationally as far away as London, England, where they received high praise at the London International Wine Fair.

The pioneer spirit that brought Tony and Edie Champ to Virginia to be a part of the fledgling Virginia wine industry has definitely paid off. They are considered among the founders of Virginia wine and rightly so, for with each vintage Tony and Edie cement their place in the rich history of Virginia wine. Indeed, for the last 20 vintages, White Hall Vineyards has shown all those who seek to follow in the path of Tony and Edie Champ how to make great wine. So the next time you are on the Monticello Wine Trail, raise your glass and toast Virginia's new pioneers.

Owner: Jerry Bias
Winemaker: Romulus Pascall
Year Established: September 2001

Est. 2001

Wisdom Oak Winery
Vision and Endurance Bring Forth Wisdom

By: Matt Brown

Although the first vines at Wisdom Oaks Winery were not planted until late 2001, the roots of owner Jerry Bias's interest in owning a vineyard go back much further. It all began when he and his close friend, Mike Taylor, started traveling the prestigious Napa and Sonoma County wine regions in California to collect the rare, small production, high-end wines that brought these regions fame.

Jerry's growing collection of California cult wine inspired him to combine his dream of retiring in Central Virginia with owning and operating a small, boutique winery in the Monticello American Viticultural Area (AVA). His professional experience working as a hedge fund manager in New York City had already familiarized him with the long hours and hard work that are necessary to establish a vineyard and winery. Deciding to build his dream in Albemarle County was an easy choice—Jerry had fallen in love with the area during his time as a student at the University of Virginia (UVa.). He continues to maintain a strong relationship with the University through his participation in U.Va's Investment Management Company.

Once the decision had been made to move forward, Jerry immediately began searching the Monticello AVA for the perfect vineyard site on which to plant a dream. Jerry worked with local vineyard experts, members of the University of Virginia's Department of Environmental Sciences, as well as the grandfather of Virginia wine, Gabriele Rausse, to find just the right site. Jerry finally found such a site a few miles south of Charlottesville. The elevation of the area where the main vineyard is now located ranges from 750 feet to 1,100 feet above sea level. The natural drainage at the site, a gift of the loamy soil, is ideal for planting grape vines. Additionally, the property is home to five natural springs, which provide a natural irrigation source. Located on four acres of the 126-acre estate in a rural area of southern Albemarle County, Wisdom Oak imparts the feeling of being much farther away from civilization than it really is. The long, gravel driveway conveys a taste of the farm life that is an important aspect of many of Virginia's wineries.

After choosing the perfect vineyard site and layout, Jerry placed his order for vines on September 6th, 2001. Then, five days later, Jerry's friend, Mike Taylor, who helped inspire Jerry to start the winery, lost his life in the attacks of 9/11. In honor of his friend, and to preserve the dream, Jerry carried on, and personally planted the first three hundred vines in the vineyards at Wisdom Oaks. During this time, before the vineyard even had a name or plans for a winery, Jerry realized that his vines were capable of producing top-quality grapes. In 2002, Wisdom Oak welcomed local winemaker and vineyard manager Dan Neumeister to the team. With Dan's help, Jerry was able to more fully develop Wisdom Oak's vineyards and take his dream to a whole new level. After selling the fruit from their first three vintages to other local winemakers Jerry moved to break ground on Wisdom Oak's winery. Starting in the fall of 2004, he and Dan custom built "the ideal boutique wine production facility" as the home for the future wines of Wisdom Oak. A unique feature of this modern winery is its "gravity flow" design—made to harness the power of gravity in moving grapes and wine throughout the facility. This design allows the preservation of the natural qualities of the grapes throughout the winemaking process. The first vintage of wine was produced in the new facility after its completion in early 2006.

Together, Jerry and Dan built a reputation for producing small quantity, high quality wines in the heart of Virginia's wine country. In early October of 2010 however, tragedy struck once more. A drunk driver hit Dan while he was on his motorcycle, robbing the 31 year old of his life. Having studied under Dan's dedicated winemaking, winemaker Romulus Pascall stepped up as Wisdom Oak's head winemaker. Pascall now continues Dan's level of dedication producing wines of excellent quality.

The wines of Wisdom Oak have won awards throughout the Commonwealth and the country. In addition to awards from the annual Governor's Cup and numerous medals from local and national wine festivals, they have also had the distinct honor of being chosen to supply wine at a State Dinner at the White House.

As a proud member of the Monticello Wine Trail, Wisdom Oak Winery is a shining example of a successful winery and vineyard and a testament to the hard work of Jerry Bias. On a deeper level, Wisdom Oak Winery and its owner have faced real tragedy in its brief existence. Its continuation in spite of hardship honors those two men by celebrating the vision and work they shared, and helped bring into being.

Appendices

Movies, Books, and Blogs of Recommendation

Movies
Vintage: A Winemaker's Year
Bottle Shock
A Good Year
Mondovino
Corked
From Ground to Glass
Sideways
The Secret of Santa Vittoria
Year of the Comet
Blood into Wine

Books
Beyond Jefferson's Vines, Leahy
War and Wine, Kladstrup
The World In A Glass: Six Drinks That Changed The World, Standage
The Judgement of Paris, Spurrier
Grand Cru, Norman
When the Rivers Ran Red, Sosnowski
The Widow Clicquot, Mazzeo
Confessions of a Wine Lover, Robinson
The Botanist and the Vintner, Campbell
The Ripening Sun, Atkinson
The Oxford Companion to Wine, Robinson
Noble Rot: A Bordeaux Wine Revolution, Echikson
Wine for Dummies, Ed McCarthy, Mary Ewing-Mulligan

Blogs and Websites

http://www.virginiawine.org
http://www.monticellowinetrail.com
http://theappellationtrail.com
http://richardleahy.com
http://www.virginiawinetime.com
http://swirlsipsnark.com
http://www.drinklocalwine.com
http://drinkwhatyoulike.wordpress.com
http://www.vinespot.blogspot.com
http://vawineinmypocket.com
http://vawinedogs.blogspot.com
http://www.vinography.com/archives/2012/01/book_
    review_the_drops_of_god_v.html

Wine Grapes Grown in Virginia

Albariño. Originally from Portugal and Spain, this white wine grape produces crisp, refreshing wines with high acidity, and lower alcohol.

Barbera. An Italian grape by origin, Barbera yields richly colored wine of medium body, low tannin, and high acidity. Often cellar-worthy, wines made from Barbera can develop over many years.

Cabernet Franc. One of the five noble grapes of Bordeaux, Cabernet Franc has found a new home in the warm climate of the Monticello AVA. This grape can be used to blend but performs well as a single varietal in Virginia. Its known for its fragrant nose and peppery finish.

Cabernet Sauvignon. This is another member of the Bordeaux grape family. Bolder than its offspring
Cabernet Franc, Cabernet Sauvignon produces dark, tannic wines with rich fruit-forward palates.

Chambourcin. Often a sweeter wine, Chambourcin is a hybrid variety planted mostly in the Mid-Atlantic region of the United States. Its known for pairing well with chocolate and chocolate based desserts.

Chardonnay. This is one of the most widely planted grapes in the world and produces wines all over the spectrum, from dry and sparkling to heavy and oaky. In Virginia, you might also encounter Chardonnay-Viognier blends.

Gewürztraminer. One of the more aromatic white varieties currently planted in Virginia, Gewürztraminer is known for its lychee fruit notes and is most often vinted as sweet wine (anywhere from off-dry, to desert wine).

Lemberger, Blaufränkisch. From the cooler climate of Austria, this grape has been producing excellent wines in the Shenandoah Valley. Its similar in profile to Pinot Noir and Gamay; medium tannins, strong acidity, and rich, fruity notes that become more complex with bottle age.

Malbec. Appreciated in Bordeaux for its blending qualities, Malbec is also being grown in Virginia to add structure, complexity, and color to Bordeaux style blends.

Merlot. One of the most famous Bordeaux grapes, Merlot has a wide winemaking potential and, in Virginia, is used to make everything from rosé to rich, full-bodied reds. Red fruit like plums, cherries, and blackcurrants are often distinguishing notes in Merlot.

Mourvedre. Red grape with a peppery aroma that is often used in blends.

Nebbiolo. An italian favorite, this high acid grape is full of tannin in its youth and makes a wine best enjoyed with some age.

Norton. Originally cultivated in Richmond, Virginia, this grape varietal is native to the U.S. and is widely planted here in Virginia.

Petit Manseng. A white grape from France, this grape is often produced into a sweet wine either via dehydration or freezing.

Petit Verdot. A bold, heavy, late-ripening Bordeaux variety, Petit Verdot (often referred to as PV), produces some of the most tannic and complex wines in the AVA. It is also used for blending.

Pinotage. A South African hybrid of Pinot Noir and Cinsault, Pinotage produces heavier red wines with flavors ranging from earthy undergrowth, to bright red fruits.

Pinot Blanc. Related to the red Pinot Noir grape, this white grape is quite versatile, producing everything from dessert wines, to full-bodied whites, to light, crisp, refreshing summer wines.

Pinot Gris, Pinot Grigio. Another relative of the Pinot Noir grape, Pinot Gris (aka Pinot Grigio) can be made into a wide variety of wines. It is best known for producing high-acid, crisp wines.

Pinot Noir. Known in France for producing some of the finest wines in the world in Burgundy (red wine) and Champagne (white wine), Pinot Noir is one of the few grapes that make excellent wines in red, rosé, and white wine categories.

Riesling. From Germany's Rhine region, this grape is known for taking on the quality of the land (terroir) and can be made to contain all amounts of residual sugar, from very dry, to very sweet.

Sangiovese. The grape of Chianti, Sangiovese is fruit forward, rich, and is an excellent food wine.

Sauvignon Blanc. The parent grape to Cabernet Sauvignon (along with Cabernet Franc), this white French grape from Bordeaux is planted widely throughout the world including here in Virginia.

Seyval Blanc. The grape has citrus element in the aroma and taste, as well as a minerality that may be compared to white Burgundy. It is often oaked and subjected to a stage of malolactic fermentation

Syrah, Shiraz. Used as a single varietal or blended, Syrah produces rich wines, with loads of fruit on the palate and nose. It's home in the Rhône Valley is not dissimilar from Central Virginia, which accounts for its success in the Commonwealth.

Traminette. A hybrid of Gewürztraminer, this grape is best known for the dessert wines it produces.

Verdejo. Known for pairing well with a variety of foods, especially Spanish cusine, Verdejo is a varietal of Spanish origin that yields a full-bodied white wine.

Verdelho. Not to be confused with Verdejo, this grape is of Portuguese origin and is often made into flinty, citrusy whites or blended with other grapes to produce the rich reds of Madeira.

Vidal Blanc. A fast ripening, cooler-climate grape, with high acidity, Vidal Blanc is often made with significant levels of residual sugar.

Viognier. The state grape of Virginia, this French variety is originally from the Rhône Valley. It is known for its floral aromas, and tropical fruit and melon notes on the palate.

©Elizabeth Flood

Wine Terms

Acidity. The level of acid in a bottle of wine. Wines with high acidity are more sour or tart in flavor.

American Viticultural Area (AVA). Designated wine growing region in the United States recognized by the Bureau of Alcohol Tobacco and Firearms (BATF).

Appellation. Name given to a determined wine-producing region.

Aroma. Scent of the wine created by the grape.

Astringent. Tasting term referring to the drying effect that tannins give to the mouth.

Balance. When the elements of the wine (fruit, tannin, sugar, and acid) harmoniously blend.

Barrel. The container in which the wine ferments and ages (often oak).

Barrique. 225-liter barrel.

Blend. A wine made from more than one type of grape.

Body. Describes the way wine feels in the mouth; either light, medium, or full bodied. Whites are usually lighter bodied than reds.

Bouquet. Complex aromas in aged wines.

Brut. Dry champagne or sparkling wines.

Character. The odor, taste, and scent of wine.

Claret. English name referring to the red wines of Bordeaux.

Complex. A multifaceted wine with balance of flavor, bouquet, texture, and aroma.

Cork taint. Wine fault caused by a flawed cork that creates a moldy odor.

Cru. Vineyard ranking.

Crush. Process of extracting juice from the grapes. This is typically done with a press.

Cuvee. Blended batch of Champagne wine.

Decanting. This is the separation of sediment of aged wine from the wine by pouring wine into a decanter. This process introduces oxygen to the wine, thus changing the chemical structure and allowing the wine to breathe.

Demi-Sec. Dry to sweet sparkling wine.

Dessert Wine. Alcohol 17-24% by adding brandy or spirits.

Dry. Tasting term denoting the opposite of sweet, caused by tannins that elicit a puckering sensation in the mouth.

Enology. The science of wine and winemaking.

Estate Bottled. Grown and produced by vineyard at winery.

Fermentation. The conversion of grape sugars, or glucose, to alcohol by yeast metabolization.

Finish. The sensation wine delivers after swallowing.

Fortified Wine. Wine that has an additional distilled spirit added to it. This stops fermentation.

Fruity. Tasting term describing wines that exhibit strong flavors and smells of fruit.

Full bodied. Wine high in alcohol and flavor.

Herbaceous. Tasting term signifying flavors and odors of herbs in wine.

Horizontal Tasting. A tasting of wines from the same vintage from different wineries.

Hybrid. Cross-pollination of grapes.

Imperial. Eight standard bottles of wine.

Jeroboam. Six standard bottles of wine.

Late Harvest. Wine made from grapes left on the vine longer to an advanced state of ripeness for a sweet wine.

Legs. Drip on the inside of the wine glass when wine is swirled.

Length. How long the flavors of wine linger in the mouth after swallowed.

Magnum. Two times the size of a standard bottle of wine.

Meritage. US name for a red Bordeaux-style blend, combining the words "Merit and Heritage."

Méthode Champenoise. Method of sparkling wine production that allows the second stage of fermentation to occur in the bottle, thus containing carbon dioxide and creating sparkle.

Must. Unfermented grape juice before it is wine.

Non-vintage. Blends from more than one vintage with no date on the label.

Nose. A tasting term describing the aromas and bouquets of a wine; how a wine smells.

Oaky. Tasting term signifying smells and flavors of toast and vanilla in wine.

Oxidation. When wine is over-exposed to the air and undergoes a chemical change, causing a stale smell and loss of freshness in the wine.

Press. Device that crushes grapes and extracts the juice during the winemaking process.

Proof. Standard for alcohol content, measured by twice the percentage of Alcohol by Volume.

Puncheon. Barrel of wine four times the size of a standard bottle.

Racking. The clarification method of moving wine from one cask to another in order to separate clear wine from the dregs that have settled.

Riddling. The process of gradually rotating bottles of sparkling wine so the solids gather in the neck of the bottle to later be removed.

Rosé. Pink wine whose distinctive color results from little contact with the red gape skins during the fermentation process.

Sec. French for dry to semi-dry wines.

Sediment. Small dark granules that settle at the bottom of an aging vessel.

Skin Contact. Process of mixing the skins with grape juice during fermentation.

Sparkling Wine. Champagne style wine produced by allowing the second process of fermentation to occur in the bottle, thus creating carbon dioxide and sparkle. This method of fermentation is known as methode champenoise.

Spicy. Tasting term used to denote smells and flavors of aromatic spices in certain wines.

Standard Bottle. 750 milliliters.

Tannins. Acid in the skin and seeds of grapes that leave a bitter, puckery, dry feeling in the mouth.

Terroir. French for soil. Also refers to unique characteristics of a vineyard's geography and environment.

Varietal. Grape recognized by the Bureau of Alcohol, Tobacco, and Firearms. In order to appear on the label, bottles must have 75% of the varietal.

Vertical Tasting. A tasting comparing wines from consecutive years.

Vinification. The process of making wine.

Vitis Vinifera. Common European grape.

Vintage Date. Harvest date of the wine in the bottle.

Viticulture. Science of grape growing.

White Riesling. German white grape.

Zinfandel. Black grape used in producing rosé, blush and red wine.

Sites consulted:
http://www.vinology.com/dictionary/index.htm
http://www.vinovagabonds.com/wines/common-wine-
    terms-2
http://www.kenswineguide.com/wine.php?word=29

Economic Impact

In 2012, Governor Bob McDonnell announced the very encouraging findings of the *2010 Economic Impact Study of Wine and Wine Grapes on the Commonwealth of Virginia*. The independent study revealed that between 2005 and 2010, wine industry jobs increased by 50%, and the economic impact increased by 106%, from $362 million to $747 million, annually. The number of wineries also increased by 49 percent in this same time period, from 129 to 193.

"The study also highlights the significant impact that tourism is having on the Virginia wine industry, with the number of wine-related tourists visiting Virginia increasing from 1 million in 2005 to 1.62 million in 2010, a 62 percent increase. Expenditures related to winery tourism are up dramatically as well, with $57 million in 2005 versus $131 million in 2010, a 130 percent increase."

The impact of this growth strengthens the areas that need it most. Todd P. Haymore, Secretary of Agriculture and Forestry, explains that "[m]ost of the investments made, jobs created, taxes generated, and tourism driven expenditures around the wine industry are in rural areas, where they are making a big impact on local economies."

From a national perspective, sales of Virginia wine reached a record high in 2011 with more than 462,000 cases sold, an 11 percent increase over the previous year. Virginia has the fifth most wineries in the nation with 210, and is also the fifth largest grape producer.

Economic Impact (cont.)

- Office of Robert F. McDonnell, February 2, 2012*

VIRGINIA WINE, WINE GRAPES AND VINEYARDS	2010 ECONOMIC IMPACT	2005 ECONOMIC IMPACT
Full-time Equivalent Jobs	4,735	3,162
Wages Paid	$156 million	$84 million
Wine Produced (Cases)	439,500	320,200
Retail Value of Virginia Wine Sold	$73 million	$45 million
Vineyard Revenue	$11 million	$8 million
Number of Wineries	193	129
Number of Grape Growers	386	262
Grape-Bearing Acres	2,700	2,000
Wine-Related Tourism Expenditures	$131 million	$57 million
Number of Wine-Related Tourists	1,618,000	1,000,000
Taxes Paid: Federal / State and Local	$42 million / $43 million	$15 million / $21 million

*http://www.governor.virginia.gov/news/viewRelease.cfm?id=1114

Top 10 Virginia Fun Wine Facts

1. Virginia is ranked #5 in the USA for wine production behind CA, WA, OR, and NY.

2. Art Garfunkel (of Simon and Garfunkel) once lived at the Edgewood Estate, current site of Keswick Vineyards.

3. During his eight years as president, Jefferson ran a personal wine bill of $10,835.90, which adjusted for inflation translates to $146,524.40. His wine collection was one of the reasons he died in debt.

4. Ducard Vineyards, in Madison, had the first solar powered tasting room in Virginia.

5. October is Virginia Wine Month.

6. Thomas Jefferson's household consumed an average of 400 bottles of wine a year.

7. There is no state law requiring workers to wash their feet before making Virginia wine.

8. Washington, DC leads the nation in terms of wine consumption.

9. Most Virginia vineyards begin harvest when the brix count (sugar content) is around 23.

10. The ABC guideline for wine is 18.9%; anything above is considered spirits.

Contact Information for Wineries

Afton Mountain Vineyards
234 Vineyard Lane
Afton, VA 22920
(540) 456-8667
www.aftonmountainvinyeards.com
finewines@aftonmountainvineyards.com
Open daily 11-6, except Tuesdays and Christmas, New
Year's Day, Thanksgiving and Easter

Barboursville Vineyards
17655 Winery Road
Barboursville, VA 22923
(540) 832-3824
www.barboursvillewine.net
bvvy@barboursvillewine.com
Open daily except Thanksgiving, Christmas Day, and New
Year's Day, from 10-5 on Monday through Saturday, and
11-5 on Sunday

Blenheim Vineyards
31 Blenheim Farm
Charlottesville, VA 22902
(434) 293-5366
www.blenheimvineyards.com
info@blenheimvineyards.com
Open daily 11-5:30

Burnley Vineyards
4500 Winery Ln.
Barboursville, VA 22923
(540) 832-2828
www.burnleywines.com
bvwinery@gmx.com
Open January- mid April, Friday-Monday 11-5
Open daily mid April- December 11-5

Cardinal Point Vineyard and Winery
9423 Batesville Road
Afton, VA 22920
(540) 456-8400
www.cardinalpointwinery.com
info@cardinalpointwinery.com
Open daily 11-5:30 except Easter, Thanksgiving,
Christmas, and New Year's Day.

DelFosse Vineyard and Winery
500 DelFosse Winery Ln
Faber, VA 22938
(434) 263-6100
www.delfossewine.com
finewines@delfossewine.com
Open Wednesday to Sunday 11-5 and Mondays and
Tuesdays by appointment

Early Mountain Vineyards
6109 Wolftown-Hood Road
Madison, Virginia 22727
(540) 948-9005
www.earlymountain.com
cheers@earlymountain.com
Open Sunday–Monday, Wednesday–Thursday 11-6 and
Friday–Saturday 11-8

First Colony Winery
1650 Harris Creek Road
Charlottesville, VA 22902
(434) 979-7105
www.firstcolonywinery.com
info@firstcolonywinery.com
Open Monday–Friday 10-5,
Saturday 11-6, Sunday 11-5

Flying Fox Vineyard
27 Chapel Hollow Road
Afton, VA 22920
(434) 361-1692
www.flyingfoxvineyard.com
info@flyingfoxvineyard.com
Open Friday–Sunday 11-5

Gabrielle Rausse
(434) 296-5328
Not open to the public.

Glass House Winery
5898 Free Union Road
Free Union, VA 22940
(434) 975-0094
www.glasshousewinery.com
michelle@glasshousewinery.com
Open Thursday- Sunday 12-5:30 and until 9 on Fridays

Grace Estate Winery
5273 Mount Juliet Farm
Crozet, VA 22932
(434) 823 1486
www.graceestatewinery.com
info@graceestatewinery.com
Open Thursday-Sunday 11-

Horton Vineyards
6399 Spotswood Trail
Gordonsville, VA 22942
(800) 829-4633
www.hortonwine.com
vawinee@aol.com
Open daily 10-5

Jefferson Vineyards
1353 Thomas Jefferson Parkway
Charlottesville, VA 22902
(434) 977-3042
www.jeffersonvineyards.com
office@jeffersonvineyards.com
Open daily 10-6

Keswick Vineyards
1575 Keswick Winery Drive
Keswick, VA 22947
(434) 244-3341
www.keswickvineyards.com
tastingroom@keswickvineyards.com
Open daily 9-5 pm

Kilauwren Winery
1543 Evergreen Church Rd.
Standardsville, VA 22973
(434) 985 2535
www.kilauwrenwinery.com
info@kilauwrenwinery.com
Open Friday-Sunday and holiday Mondays 12-5

King Family Vineyards
6550 Roseland Farm
Crozet, VA 22932
(434) 823-7800
www.kingfamilyvineyards.com
Open Daily from 10:30-5:30

Lovingston Winery
885 Freshwater Cove Ln.
Lovingston, VA 22949
(434) 263-8467
www.lovingstonwinery.com
Open April-November: Wednesday-Friday 10-4, Saturday
and Sunday 11-5.
December- March: by appointment

Moss Vineyards
1849 Simmons Gap Road
Nortonsville, VA 22935
(434) 823-7605
www.mossvineyards.net
mossvineyards@gmail.com
Open Friday-Sunday 12-5

Mountfair Vineyards
4875 Mountain Road
Crozet, VA 22932
(434) 823- 7605
www.mountfair.com
info@mountfair.com
Open Friday-Sunday 12-6

Pippin Hill Farm and Vineyards
5022 Plank Road
North Garden, VA 22959
(434) 202-8063
www.pippinhillfarm.com
info@pippinhillfarm.com
Open Tuesday-Sunday 11-5

Pollak Vineyards
330 Newtown Road
Greenwood, VA 22943
(540) 456-8844
www.pollakvineyards.com
info@pollakvineyards.com
Open daily April-October 11-5
Open November-March, Wednesday-Sunday 11-5
Closed Thanksgiving, Christmas and New Year's Day

Prince Michel Vineyard and Winery
154 Winery Lane
Leon, Virginia 22725
(540) 547-3707
www.princemichel.com
info@princemichel.com
Open daily 10-6

Reynard Florence Vineyard
16109 Burnley Rd.
Barboursville, VA 22973
(540) 832-3895
info@reynardflorence.com
Open Saturday and Sunday 11-5

Stinson Vineyards
4744 Sugar Hollow Rd.
Crozet, VA 22932
(434) 823-7300
www.stinstonvineyards.com
info@stinsonvineyards.com
Open Thursday-Sunday 11-5 or by appointment

Stone Mountain Vineyards
1376 Wyatt Mountain Road
Dyke, VA 22935
(434) 990 9463
www.stonemountainvineyards.com
info@stonemountainvineyards.com
Open March-Mid December, Friday-Sunday 11-5

Trump Winery
3550 Blenheim Road
Charlottesville, VA 22902
(434) 977-3895

Veritas Vineyard and Winery
151 Veritas Lane
Afton, Virginia 22920
(540) 456-8000
www.veritaswines.com
contact@veritaswines.com
Open Monday-Friday 9:30-5:30 and Saturday and Sunday
11-5. Closed on Thanksgiving, Christmas and
New Year's Day

Virginia Wineworks
1781 Harris Creek Way
Charlottesville, VA 22902
(434) 296-3438
www.virginiawineworks.com
info@virginiawineworks.com
Open daily 11-5

Well Hung Vineyard
(434) 260-1501
www.wellhungvineyard.com
info@wellhungvineyard.com
Private

White Hall Vineyards
5190 Sugar Ridge Rd.
Crozet, VA 22932
(434) 823-8615
www.whitehallvineyards.com
tastingroom@whitehallvineyards.com
Open Wednesday-Sunday 11-5

Wisdom Oak Winery
3613 Walnut Branch Lane
North Garden, VA 22959
(434) 984-4272
www.wisdomoakwinery.com
info@wisdomoakwinery.com
Open Thursday-Sunday 12-6

Contributor's Bios

Andrea Saathoff | Author

Andrea Saathoff earned her B.A. at the University of Notre Dame and M.A. at Michigan State, and has lived with her family in Virginia for the last three decades. After an extensive career in education, she founded Albemarle Limousine and Blue Ridge Wine Excursions in 2008 with the goal of offering a luxury transportation service to the Albemarle community and its visitors.

She and her team focus on excellence in customer service, and hosting guests as they explore the best that Virginia has to offer. Her team of exceptional Virginians strive to offer the best wine tour experience and transportation service in the region.

When visiting central Virginia, expect to see Andrea continuing to explore the Monticello Wine Trail!

Chris Campanelli | Contributing Editor, Writer

Chris graduated from the University of Virginia in 2007 as a history major. Since joining the team, Chris has become a vital part of Blue Ridge Wine Excursions, both as a trail guide, and as our Brew Trail Development Coordinator. When not involved in the world of food, Chris is playing music and traveling with one of three bands: Camp Christopher, The Hill and Wood, and Nettles. Chris released his first album, *Beyond the Word*, in 2012.

Andy Josselyn | Editor, Contributing Writer

Andy Josselyn had his first sip of wine sitting under a particularly large Gum tree listening to Koalas mate above. It sounded terrifying, but tasted *delicious*.

Multiple love affairs were consummated that night, and Andy has been enamored with drinking wine in pretty places ever since. He enjoys helping others find a passion for Virginia wine out on the Monticello Wine Trail as a guide at Blue Ridge. He is also the Editor at Large of an Australian short story magazine called *The Canary Press*, which is actively (and successfully) avoiding any association with the word prestigious.

Boo Barnett | Contributing Writer

So Virginian that some of her ancestors met the first boats at Jamestown, Boo Barnett began giving local tours for a Girl Scout badge. Having worked in regional, state and international presentations for decades, she loves introducing the worlds of Virginia wines and local history to visitors and new residents alike. Her familiarity with the owners and their specialties allows her to design a tour around your personal preferences, whether that leads to historical cideries, celebrity tasting rooms or anything in between. When not overseeing her organic farm or tending her beagle rescue group, Boo can be found picnicking with friends at her favorite wineries. Salud!

Matt Brown | Contributing Writer

Originally from Roanoke, Virginia, Matthew Brown graduated from the University of Virginia in 2010 with a degree in Foreign Affairs. Matthew works full time at King Family Vineyards in Crozet, where he enjoys staffing the tasting room year-round, conducting private tastings and tours of the winery, and getting his hands dirty in the vineyard during harvest time. Matthew has also served as the Wine Trail Program Developer for Blue Ridge Wine Excursions, where he relied on his experience in researching and selling wines and working in vineyards to help him craft exceptional Monticello Wine Trail tours. His dream is to one day own his own vineyard here in Virginia.

Gayle Davies | Contributing Writer

Gayle has been involved in the wine industry in both California and Virginia for twenty years, working at different wineries and as a Wine Trail Guide for Blue Ridge Wine Excursions. She recently became a Certified Specialist of Wine, which is recognized by the Society of Wine Educators. In addition to her interest in local wines, Gayle has become a part of the locavore movement in Charlottesville, which showcases the plethora of food that Charlottesville has to offer. She and her husband operate a local store in Belmont called The Farm.

Bit Pressley | Contributing Editor, Writer

Bit, originally from Atlanta Georgia, graduated from Pace University and University of North Carolina.
Bit enjoys working with Blue Ridge Wine Excursions because it gives him a chance to combine two great passions: American history and Virginia wine.

No tour is complete with Bit until he has shared some of the history of Charlottesville and entertained you with colorful stories about historical characters and local customs.

Justin Stone | Contributing Writer

Justin, a wine, beer and local food expert, is an active Blue Ridge Wine Excursions Trail Guide. After graduating from the University of Virginia in 2009, Justin split his time between teaching high school students and pouring wine for jovial festival-goers across the state of Virginia—a job that began his joyful pursuit of wine. Along with continuing his involvement in the local wine industry, Justin co-runs a grassroots dinner series called Forage with a close friend in the culinary arts, and works as an Account Manager in the university division of WorldStrides.

Eric Bryant | Production, Artistic Design

In 2010 Eric became a critical member of the Blue Ridge Wine Excursions team and has overseen the reserving and execution of nearly 2000 corporate shuttles, airport transfers, weddings, and Virginia Wine Tours. Prior to Albemarle Limousine, he worked as a Certified Massage Therapist at the University of Virginia Aquatics and Fitness Center and traveled with the U.Va Men and Women's swim teams. In addition to his interest in health and fitness and his natural affinity for helping others, Eric operates a boutique videography company, Unboxed Productions.

Mike Uriss | Graphic Art

Mike is an award-winning artist and art instructor of thirty years, working in traditional and digital media. On the traditional side, he draws, paints and has taught at UVA SCPS, PVCC, the Senior Center of Charlottesville, and summer programs for the Curry School at UVA and Tandem Friends School. Mike has shown digital art in Tokyo, the Boston Museum of Contemporary Art, and International University, San Diego. His commercial art is implemented by groups ranging from start-ups to Fortune 500 companies. He studied at the School of the Art Institute of Chicago, Platt College in San Diego, the University of Virginia, and holds a BA in fine art from Mary Baldwin College. Having raised two sons in Charlottesville, Mike continues to hone his skills here in Central Virginia.

Elizabeth Flood | Artist, Research Assistant

Elizabeth is a History and Religious Studies major, class of 2014 at the University of Virginia. For the past three years, she has worked with Blue Ridge Wine Excursions where she plays a crucial role in organizing wine tours and transportation and enjoys learning the ropes of entrepreneurship. Elizabeth also works as BRWE's artist in residence, and contributed the cover illustration and pencil drawings for this publication. Having recently studied abroad in Siena, Italy, she brings knowledge of Tuscan food and wine to Virginia. Outside of the classroom, Elizabeth enjoys hiking near Charlottesville, playing ultimate Frisbee, and painting.

Mary Flood | Research Assistant

Mary is an Education and History major, class of 2014 at the University of Virginia. Mary has been a part of Blue Ridge Excursions for three years and plays an integral role in organizing wine tours and working as a "creator of order." After spending the summer in Tuscany studying food, wine and Italian culture, she gained a greater appreciation for all the wineries that the Monticello Wine Trail has to offer. When not packing picnic baskets or writing history papers, Mary spends her time exploring Charlottesville's local hiking trails, cuisine, and music scene.

A portion of the proceeds for sales of this guide will go to support *ParadeRest*, a local 501(c)(3).

Like many communities around the country, Central Virginia is home to the National Guard, Reservists and their families. Without a nearby veterans hospital or military base, the sacrifices of those serving in the wars in Iraq and Afghanistan are often unrecognized. Many organizations in our region such as The Paramount Theater, U.Va, and Blue Ridge Wine Excursions wish to express their gratitude by inviting service members to be guests at their performances, special events and programs.

ParadeRest launched with the assistance of the American Red Cross, Blue Star Families, and Research Strategies Network. ParadeRest encourages expressions of our community's gratitude to veterans, soon-to-be-deployed service members, and their families.

For more information, please visit:
www.paraderest.org

Made in the USA
Lexington, KY
27 May 2018